D0165075

F|O|C|U|S
ON PRONUNCIATION 2

LINDA LANE

American Language Program
Columbia University

Longman

Focus on Pronunciation 2

Copyright © 2005 by Linda Lane.
All rights reserved.
No part of this publication may be reproduced,
stored in a retrieval system, or transmitted
in any form or by any means, electronic, mechanical,
photocopying, recording, or otherwise,
without the prior permission of the publisher.

Pearson Education, 10 Bank Street, White Plains, NY 10606

Executive editor: Laura Le Dréan
Associate acquisitions editor: Dena Daniel
Development editor: Dana Klinek
Marketing manager: Joe Chapple
Production coordinator: Melissa Leyva
Senior manufacturing buyer: Nancy Flaggman
Cover and text design: Pat Wosczyk
Cover photo: © Dimitri Veritsiotis/Digital Vision, Ltd.
Project management and text composition: Elm Street Publishing Services, Inc.
Text font: 11.5/13 Minion
Pronunciation diagrams: Tracey Cataldo
Text art: Jill Wood

Library of Congress Cataloging-in-Publication Data

Lane, Linda (Linda L.)
    Focus on pronunciation. 2 / Linda Lane.
      p. cm.
    ISBN 0-13-097877-9
    1. English language—Pronunciation—Problems, exercises, etc. 2. English
language—Textbooks for foreign speakers. I. Title: FOP1. II. Title.
PE1137.L22 2005
428.3'4—dc22   2004008145

ISBN: 0-13-097877-9

LONGMAN ON THE **WEB**

Longman.com offers online resources for teachers
and students. Access our Companion Websites, our
online catalog, and our local offices around the world.

Visit us at **longman.com**.

Printed in the United States of America
6 7 8 9 10 11 12 13—VHG—12 11 10 09 08

CONTENTS

ABOUT *FOCUS ON PRONUNCIATION 2*

Focus on Pronunciation 2 is a comprehensive course that helps intermediate students speak English more clearly and accurately. The course covers all aspects of pronunciation—sounds, stress, rhythm, and intonation.

ORGANIZATION OF *FOCUS ON PRONUNCIATION 2*

The units of *Focus on Pronunciation 2* are organized in four parts: Vowels, Consonants, Stress in Words, and Rhythm and Intonation. Each part begins with an overview unit. The overview unit presents important topics included in that part. The units following the overview deal in depth with specific pronunciation points.

The Self-Study section provides listening and pronunciation practice. It usually includes one or more controlled exercises and a freer speaking task. This section is to be recorded by the student for the teacher to review and comment on.

UNIT ORGANIZATION

The units following the overviews typically have the following organization:

INTRODUCTION

The Introduction presents and explains the pronunciation point. It may show how sounds are made or present other useful information on the pronunciation point. Its purpose is to make students aware of the pronunciation point.

FOCUSED PRACTICE

This section contains classroom practice activities. The activities are designed to ensure student involvement through games, interactive tasks, and listening/ speaking activities dealing with high-interest topics.

- Students first work on controlled activities that allow them to develop skill and proficiency with the particular point.
- They then practice the point in freer, communicative activities. When students are engaged in the freer activities, they should be encouraged to keep in mind these global features of clear speaking:
  - Speak Slowly
  - Speak Loudly Enough
  - Pay Attention to the Ends of Words
  - Use Your Voice to Speak Expressively

AUDIO

The Classroom audio program for *Focus on Pronunciation 2* has all the recorded activities for the course. In addition, there are Student CDs containing the Self-Study exercises.

KEY TO ICONS

🎧 —material recorded on the full audio program

🎧 —material recorded on the Student CDs

👤 —pair activity

👥 —group activity

📼 —material for students to record and give to the teacher

PLANNING A SYLLABUS

The units in *Focus on Pronunciation 2* can be used in any order. In my own teaching, I like to "skip around"—for example, teaching the overview unit for Vowels, then a specific vowel unit, then the overview for Stress in Words, then a specific unit from Stress in Words, and so on. Teachers who adopt this approach could also cover all the overview units at the beginning of the course and then skip around within the sections. The units can also be taught in order, first covering vowels, then consonants, and so on.

REFERENCES

The following research influenced the content and method of this book.

Avery, Peter and S. Ehrlich. *Teaching American English Pronunciation.* Oxford: Oxford University Press, 1992.

Celce-Murcia, Marianne, D. M. Brinton, and J. M. Goodwin. *Teaching Pronunciation: A Reference for Teachers of English to Speakers of Other Languages.* Cambridge: Cambridge University Press, 1996.

Dauer, Rebecca. *Accurate English.* Prentice Hall Regents, 1993.

ACKNOWLEDGMENTS

I am indebted to a number of people whose support, patience, and good humor made this book possible. I am grateful for the help and suggestions of my editors at Pearson: Ginny Blanford, Laura Le Dréan, Sylvia Bloch, Dena Daniel, Dana Klinek, Paula Van Ells, and Helen Ambrosio.

I am grateful for the insightful comments and suggestions of the reviewers: Cindy Chang, University of Washington, Seattle, WA; Ninah Beliavsky, St. John's University, Jamaica, NY; Lauren Randolph, Rutgers University, Piscataway, NJ; Robert Baldwin, UCLA, Los Angeles, CA.

I would also like to express my thanks to my colleagues at the American Language Program at Columbia University, who used these materials in their own classes, for their advice and feedback.

For the encouragement and patience of my family, Mile, Martha, Sonia, and Luke, and of my dear friend Mary Jerome, I am deeply grateful.

Finally, I want to thank my students—for teaching me how they learn pronunciation, for wanting to improve their pronunciation, and for showing me how to help them.

Linda Lane

ABOUT THE AUTHOR

Linda Lane is a faculty member in the American Language Program of Columbia University. She is coordinator of Columbia's TESOL Certificate Program, where she also teaches Applied Phonetics and Pronunciation Teaching and Introduction to Second Language Acquisition. She received her Ed.D. in Applied Linguistics from Teachers College, Columbia University, and her M.A. in Linguistics from Yale University.

VOWELS

UNIT 1 Vowel overview

INTRODUCTION

🎧 There are eleven vowels and three complex vowels in English. Listen.

		Front	Central	Back
High	Tense	[iy] heat		[uw] tooth
	Relaxed	[ɪ] hit		[ʊ] took
Mid	Tense	[ey] hate	[ə] cut	[ow] coat
	Relaxed	[ɛ] head		
Low		[æ] hat		[ɔ] caught
			[ɑ]hot	

Look at the diagram. Different positions of the tongue create different vowel sounds. For example, when you say the vowel in *hot,* your tongue is low, in the center of your mouth.

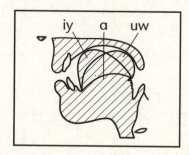

🎧 There are three complex vowels, called "diphthongs." Listen.

[ay]	[aw]	[oy]
eye	how	boy

FOCUSED PRACTICE

1 SEEING AND FEELING VOWELS

Work with a partner. Say the following word combinations slowly. Your partner will describe your lips and mouth as you change from word to word. (You can also do this by yourself with a mirror.)

1. *hot-heat-hot-heat* (What happens as you go from *hot* to *heat*?)

 Hot Your mouth is open.

2. *see-Sue-see-Sue-see-Sue* (What happens as you go from *see* to *Sue*?)

3. *day-do-day-do* (What happens as you go from *day* to *do*?)

2 HEARING THE ENDS OF VOWELS

The vowels [iy], [ey], [uw], and [ow] end in a short [y] or [w] sound, called "glides." The glide is not always shown in the spelling. When another vowel follows [iy], [ey], [uw], or [ow], use the glide to join the two vowels.

Listen to these phrases and repeat them. Join the words together.

[iy]	[ey]	[uw]	[ow]
1. see ͮus	3. say͜ it	5. do ͮit	7. go ͮup
2. be ͮover	4. pay͜ Ann	6. too ͮeasy	8. show͜ us

3 TENSE AND RELAXED VOWELS

A. Listen to these words and look at the mouth pictures. Repeat the words.

Tense Vowels   **Relaxed Vowels**

sheep [iy]   ship [ɪ]

paper [ey]   pepper [ɛ]

Luke [uw]   look [ʊ]

VOWEL OVERVIEW   3

B. Look at the pictures of the tense and relaxed pairs of vowels in Part A. Complete the sentences with the correct words.

1. When you say the tense vowel [iy], your lips are _____ (spread/relaxed).

2. When you say [ɪ], your lips are _____ (spread/relaxed).

3. Your lips are _____ (more/less) rounded for [uw] than for [ʊ].

---

4 LISTEN FOR DIFFERENCES: *Vowels*

🎧 **A. Listen to these words and repeat them.**

1. a. seen	4. a. pool	7. a. daily
b. sin	b. pull	b. deli
2. a. Luke	5. a. taste	8. a. each
b. look	b. test	b. itch
3. a. wait	6. a. sheep	9. a. who'd
b. wet	b. ship	b. hood

🎧 **B. Listen again and circle the words you hear.**

---

5 DICTATIONS

Work with a partner. Read sentences to your partner. Your partner will write what you say (don't show your sentences to your partner). Then your partner will read sentences to you. Student A's sentences are on page 191. Student B's sentences are on page 194.

---

6 WORD GROUPS: *TV programs*

🎧 **A. Listen to these words and repeat them.**

shopping shows	dramas	quiz shows	comedies
action movies	classic movies	news	history shows
food shows	cartoons		

B. The underlined letters in Part A have [ɪ], [uw], [ɑ], or [æ] sounds. Write each word in the correct column.

[ɪ] hit	[uw] tooth	[ɑ] hot	[æ] hat
_____	_____	shopping	_____
_____	_____	_____	_____
_____	_____	_____	_____
_____	_____	_____	_____

C. Work with a partner. Write examples of these types of TV shows.

1. Quiz shows: _Jeopardy_ _____

2. Situation comedies: _____

3. Dramas: _____

4. News: _____

5. Cartoons: _____

D. Work with a partner. Talk about your TV-watching habits. Write your answers in the chart.

	Name: _____	**Name:** _____
How much TV do you watch a week?		
What shows do you like to watch?		
Do you snack while you watch TV?		
When the TV is on, do you watch it or do you use it for background noise while you do something else?		

UNIT 2 [iy] sheep and [ɪ] ship

INTRODUCTION

- Many languages have a vowel similar to the vowel in *sheep*.
- The vowel in *ship* is a new vowel for many students.

Look at the pictures. They show you how to say the sounds [iy] and [ɪ].

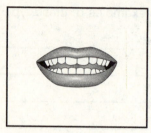 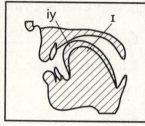 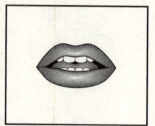

[iy] sheep, leave

Spread your lips.
End the vowel with
a [y] sound.

[ɪ] ship, live

Relax your lips.
Lower your tongue
a little.

- When [iy] is followed by another vowel, use [y] to join the two vowels.

    radi^yo   see^ya movie

Spellings for [iy]	Spellings for [ɪ]

Common
    ee: need, feet, succeed, see
    ie: believe, piece, movie
    ei: receive
    ea: mean, east, eat
    i: police, ski, machine
Other
    e: people, key, medium
	Common
	    i (between consonants): sit,
	       ship, listen, give
	Other
	    u: busy, business
	    ui: build, guilty
	    y: gym
	Unusual
	    women

FOCUSED PRACTICE

1 LISTEN AND PRACTICE: Words with [iy] and [ɪ]

🎧 Listen to these words and repeat them.

	[iy]						[ɪ]
1.	E	5.	be	9.	ship	13.	busy
2.	sheep	6.	leave	10.	middle	14.	women
3.	believe	7.	reason	11.	live	15.	rich
4.	machine	8.	people	12.	minute	16.	miss

2 LISTEN FOR DIFFERENCES: [iy] versus [ɪ]

🎧 A. Listen to these words and repeat them.

1.	a. eat	3.	a. heel	5.	a. reason	7.	a. deed
	b. it		b. hill		b. risen		b. did
2.	a. steal	4.	a. sheep	6.	a. leave	8.	a. each
	b. still		b. ship		b. live		b. itch

🎧 B. Listen again and circle the words you hear.

3 BINGO: Words with [iy] and [ɪ]

🎧 A. Listen to the words on the Bingo card and repeat them. Write [iy] or [ɪ] under each word.

1. reason *[iy]*	5. ship	9. live	13. heel
2. it	6. each	10. fit	14. sheep
3. hill	7. risen	11. rich	15. leave
4. itch	8. feet	12. reach	16. eat

B. Now play Bingo. Use the card in Part A. Listen carefully and cross out each word you hear. When you have crossed out a complete row or column , say "Bingo!"

4 SOUNDS AND SPELLING

A. Listen to these words and repeat them.

1. live	5. bead	9. eat	13. deep
2. leave	6. busy	10. build	14. give
3. rhythm	7. police	11. medium	15. gym
4. reason	8. listen	12. ship	16. chief

B. Look at the words in Part A. Write each word in the correct column.

[iy]	[ɪ]
leave	*live*
_____	_____
_____	_____
_____	_____
_____	_____
_____	_____
_____	_____
_____	_____

5 SAYING SENTENCES

A. Listen to these sentences and repeat them.

1. Miss Meese received her picture of six eagles sitting on three igloos.

2. Steven Stivens reached for a dish of rich ice cream.

3. On the weekend, the women go swimming in the swift, deep river.

4. Jim's jeep skidded on the slippery street during the sleet storm.

5. Does the criminal still steal political secrets?

B. Work in small groups. Take turns reading a sentence to the group.

6 DIFFERENCES IN MEANING

Work with a partner. Take turns asking each other to define one of the words below. Pronounce the vowel carefully so your partner knows which definition to read to you.

EXAMPLE

What does "leave" mean?

"Leave" means the opposite of "stay."

Words		Definitions
1.	**a.** leave	the opposite of "stay"
	b. live	the opposite of "die"
2.	**a.** rich	wealthy
	b. reach	to extend the arm to get something
3.	**a.** ship	a large boat
	b. sheep	a woolly animal
4.	**a.** fill	to put things in a container
	b. feel	to touch something

7 JOIN VOWELS TOGETHER: [iy] + *another vowel*

- When [iy] is followed by another vowel, use [y] to join the two vowels together.

Listen to these words and phrases, and repeat them. Use [y] to join the underlined vowels together. The letter "y" has been added to help you say the words correctly.

1. radi^yo
2. pi^yano
3. rainy afternoon
4. re^yalize
5. ide^ya
6. see^y it
7. be^y a doctor
8. seri^yous
9. medi^yum

Steven Stivens is from Boulder, Colorado. He's leaving home to go to college in Miami, Florida. Silvia Seely is from Miami. She's decided to go to college in Boulder. They both love their hometowns, but they want to live in another part of the country for a while. They know they're going to miss their hometowns.

🎧 **A.** Listen to the words and phrases in the box and repeat them. The bold letters are [iy] or [ɪ].

palm tr**ee**s	sk**ii**ng	b**ea**ch
sw**i**mming	sn**o**w	fresh s**ea**food
w**i**nter	mountains	change of s**ea**sons
snow board**i**ng	Cuban cuis**i**ne	P**e**ter (Steven's best friend)
B**i**ll (Silvia's boyfriend)		

B. What will Steven and Silvia miss when they go to college? Write each word from Part A in the correct column.

Steven will miss . . .

skiing

_____

_____

_____

_____

_____

Silvia will miss . . .

_____

_____

_____

_____

_____

C. Check your answers with a partner. Practice making sentences about Silvia and Steven.

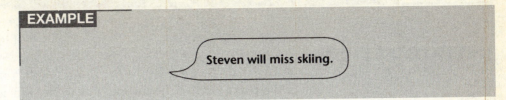

EXAMPLE

Steven will miss skiing.

9 INTERVIEWS: *What do they miss?*

 Find two students who have had to leave their hometowns or countries. Ask them what they miss. Write their names and what they miss in the chart.

Names	What do you miss?
1.	
2.	

SELF-STUDY

🎧 **First listen to:**

• the words in Exercises 1 and 2.

📼 **Now record them.**

How are your [iy] and [ɪ] sounds?

Then make a one-minute recording. Describe a place you had to leave. What do you miss about the place? What don't you miss?

UNIT 3 [ey] late, [ɛ] let, and [ɪ] lit

INTRODUCTION

Look at the pictures. They show you how to say the sounds [ey], [ɛ], and [ɪ].

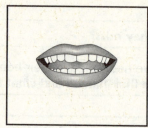 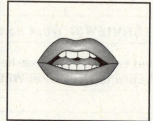 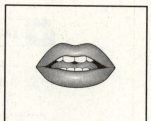

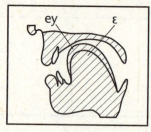 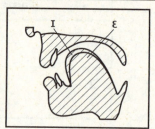

[ey] late, pain	[ɛ] let, pen	[ɪ] lit, pin
Spread your lips. End [ey] with a [y] sound.	Don't spread your lips as much. Your mouth is more open for [ɛ] than for [ey].	Don't spread your lips. Your mouth is more closed for [ɪ] than for [ɛ].

Spellings for [ey]	Spellings for [ɛ]
Common aC(C)e (C is a consonant; e is silent): face, name, make, taste ai, ay: wait, rain, day, play Other ei: rein, eight, neighbor ey: they, convey ea: break, great	Common eC(C) (C is a consonant): let, get, egg, best air: chair, hair, air ead: bread, head, instead Other ai: again, said, against ea: breakfast, heavy, weather
Spellings for [ɪ]: See Unit 2.	

12   UNIT 3

FOCUSED PRACTICE

1 LISTEN AND PRACTICE: *Words with* [ey] *and* [ɛ]

🎧 Listen to these words and repeat them.

	[ey]				[ɛ]		
1.	late	5.	make	9.	let	13.	guess
2.	age	6.	afraid	10.	healthy	14.	breakfast
3.	break	7.	name	11.	question	15.	pepper
4.	wait	8.	weight	12.	said	16.	friend

2 LISTEN FOR DIFFERENCES: [ɪ] *versus* [ɛ]

🎧 A. Listen to these words and repeat them.

1.	a.	Sid	3.	a.	sit	5.	a.	big	7.	a.	bitter
	b.	said		b.	set		b.	beg		b.	better

2.	a.	pin	4.	a.	hear	6.	a.	fill	8.	a.	lid
	b.	pen		b.	hair		b.	fell		b.	led

🎧 B. Listen again and circle the words you hear.

3 LISTEN FOR DIFFERENCES: [ey] *versus* [ɛ] *versus* [ɪ]

🎧 A. Listen to these words and repeat them.

1.	a.	mate	4.	a.	sail
	b.	met		b.	sell
	c.	mitt*		c.	sill*

2.	a.	pain	5.	a.	H
	b.	pen		b.	etch*
	c.	pin		c.	itch

3.	a.	late	6.	a.	takes
	b.	let		b.	Tex
	c.	lit		c.	ticks

mitt: baseball glove; *sill*: bottom flat part of a window; *etch*: cut designs into metal

[ey] LATE, [ɛ] LET, AND [ɪ] LIT   13

B. Listen again and circle the words you hear.

C. Work with a partner. Take turns saying one of the words in Part A. Your partner will tell you which word you said.

4 BINGO: *Words with* [ey], [ɛ], *and* [ɪ]

A. Listen to the words on the Bingo card and repeat them. Write [ey], [ɛ], or [ɪ] under each word.

1. pain *[ey]*	5. edge	9. sailor	13. mitt	17. pen
2. met	6. fill	10. pin	14. fell	18. wet
3. lit	7. wait	11. hair	15. let	19. mate
4. age	8. late	12. fail	16. head	20. seller

B. Now play Bingo. Use the card in Part A. Listen carefully and cross out each word you hear. When you have crossed out a complete row or column , say "Bingo!"

5 SAYING SENTENCES

A. Listen to these sentences and repeat them.

1. The rain wrecked the rake that Rick left on the road.

2. Tex is taking ticks out of Tessie's tame terrier.

3. How late will you let me keep the light lit?

4. The silly salesman sold sails to seven sailors.

5. The man with the mitt met the first mate.

B. Work in small groups. Take turns reading a sentence to the group.

---

6 LISTENING: *New Year's resolutions*

The new year is a time to make a fresh start. In January, many people decide to improve their health, their financial situation, and their personal lives.

Listen to these New Year's resolutions. Write the resolutions in the blanks.

I'm going to . . .

1. _____*lose*_____ _____*weight*_____.
2. _____ _____ of _____.
3. _____ _____ _____.
4. _____ _____ _____.
5. _____ _____.
6. _____ _____ _____ with my
   _____ and _____.
7. _____ a _____ _____.
8. _____ _____ TV.
9. _____ more _____.
10. _____ _____.

---

7 INTERVIEWS: *What were your New Year's resolutions?*

Work in small groups. Talk about New Year's resolutions. Were people successful in keeping their resolutions? Discuss why or why not.

🎧 **First listen to:**

- the words in Exercises 1 and 3.

📼 **Now record them.**

Then make a short recording about New Year's resolutions.

Answer some of these questions:

- Do you make New Year's resolutions?
- If you make them, what are some resolutions you've made?
- Have you been able to keep them?
- Do people in your country make New Year's resolutions?

UNIT 4 [æ] black and [ɛ] red

INTRODUCTION

Look at the pictures. They show you how to say the sounds [æ] and [ɛ].

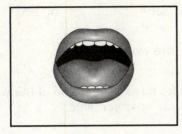

[æ] black, sad

Open your mouth and spread your lips.
The tip of your tongue is behind your bottom teeth.

[ɛ] red, said

Your mouth is more closed for [ɛ] than for [æ].

Spellings for [æ]	Spellings for [ɛ]
Common aC(C) (C is a consonant): glad, hat, past, hand **Other** au: laugh ai: plaid	See Unit 3.

FOCUSED PRACTICE

I   LISTEN AND PRACTICE: *Words with* [æ]

🎧 Listen to these words and repeat them.

1. black	4. matter	7. hat	10. exactly
2. relax	5. answer	8. happen	11. plant
3. bad	6. grass	9. magic	12. national

2 | LISTEN FOR DIFFERENCES: [æ] *versus* [ɛ]

🎧 **A. Listen to these words and repeat them.**

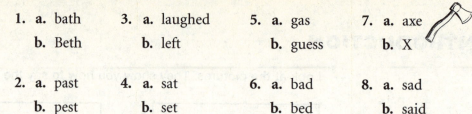

1. **a.** bath   3. **a.** laughed   5. **a.** gas   7. **a.** axe
   b. Beth   **b.** left   **b.** guess   **b.** X

2. **a.** past   4. **a.** sat   6. **a.** bad   8. **a.** sad
   b. pest   **b.** set   **b.** bed   **b.** said

🎧 **B. Listen again and circle the words you hear.**

👥 **C. Work with a partner. Take turns saying one of the words in Part A. Your partner will tell you which word you said.**

3 | DIFFERENCES IN MEANING

Work with a partner and take turns. Read either sentence *a* or sentence *b* to your partner. Pronounce the underlined word carefully so your partner can read the correct response to you.

Sentences	**Responses**
1. **a.** That's an unusual <u>X</u>.	Yes, it looks more like a *W*.
b. That's an unusual <u>axe</u>.	It's from my collection of antique tools.
2. **a.** After I told him the story, he <u>laughed</u>.	It was a very funny story.
b. After I told him the story, he <u>left</u>.	He had a doctor's appointment.
3. **a.** I need a <u>tan</u>.	I think you look just fine.
b. I need a <u>ten</u>.	Well, don't ask me—you still owe me twenty dollars from last week.
4. **a.** My <u>pan</u> is no good.	Another excuse not to cook!
b. My <u>pen</u> is no good.	Another excuse not to write that letter!

A. Before you listen, make sure you understand these words.

| rabbit | wedding | bouquet | spirit | anthropologists | insurance |

B. Read the situations below. Each one is associated with a superstitious belief. The bold letters are [æ] or [ɛ].

____ 1. a black cat crossing your path

____ 2. carrying a rabbit's foot

____ 3. breaking a mirror

____ 4. knocking on wood

____ 5. walking under a ladder

____ 6. finding a four-leaf clover

____ 7. throwing salt over your left shoulder

____ 8. carrying a baby upstairs

____ 9. being born on Sunday

____ 10. the bride and groom seeing each other before the wedding ceremony

____ 11. wearing garlic around your neck

____ 12. throwing the wedding bouquet

____ 13. throwing rice at the couple after the wedding

____ 14. opening the doors and windows after a person's death

____ 15. a howling dog

____ 16. carrying a silver dollar

____ 17. finding a penny

____ 18. the number 13

____ 19. Friday the 13th

____ 20. the number 4

C. Now listen and check the situations in Part B that you hear.

D. Work in small groups. Discuss the following questions:

- Do the situations that you checked in Part B involve good luck or bad luck? Do they predict something that will or will not happen?
- What about the other situations in the list? Do you know what superstitions are associated with them? (You can check the Answer Key on page 190.)

SELF-STUDY

First listen to:

- the words in Exercises 1 and 2.

Now record them.

Then make a short recording answering these questions:

- What superstitions do people in your country have?
- Do you consider yourself a superstitious person? Why or why not?

INTRODUCTION

- [ə] is the most common vowel in English. It is the sound of most unstressed vowels.

Look at the picture. It shows you how to say the sound [ə].

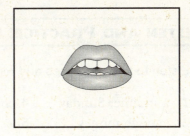

[ə] cup, money

Your mouth is almost closed.
Your tongue rests in the center of your mouth.

- The English "hesitation word" *uh* is the vowel [ə].

The restaurant is . . . uh . . . uh . . . I think it's on State Street.

Spellings for [ə]	

Common
u (between consonants): c**u**p, l**u**ck, s**u**dden, d**u**ll, h**u**ngry, st**u**ff
Other
o: m**o**ney, s**o**me, l**o**ve, **o**nce, g**o**vernment, disc**o**ver
ou: c**ou**ntry, t**ou**gh, en**ou**gh, t**ou**ch, tr**ou**ble, y**ou**ng
oe: d**oe**s, d**oe**sn't
a: wh**a**t, w**a**s
oo: bl**oo**d, fl**oo**d
	Same spelling, different sounds:
	o: m**o**nkey [ə] d**o**nkey [ɑ]
	  d**o**ne, **o**ne [ə] al**o**ne, st**o**ne [ow]
	ou: r**ou**gh [ə] alth**ou**gh [ow]
	  thr**ou**gh [uw] b**ou**ght, s**ou**ght [ɔ]
	oo: fl**oo**d, bl**oo**d [ə] f**oo**d, m**oo**d [uw]
	  g**oo**d, w**oo**d, h**oo**d [ʊ]
	Different spellings, same sound:
	o, u: s**o**n, s**u**n [ə]
	u, ou: **u**s, jeal**ou**s [ə]

FOCUSED PRACTICE

1 LISTEN AND PRACTICE: *Words with* [ə]

Listen to these words and repeat them. Your mouth should be almost closed when you say [ə].

1. son	4. number	7. country	10. dull
2. once	5. wasn't	8. doesn't	11. money
3. love	6. thumb	9. cup	12. blood

2 LISTEN AND PRACTICE: *Phrases with* [ə]

Listen to these phrases and repeat them.

1. a summer Sunday	4. my younger brother	7. does or doesn't
2. enough money	5. a sudden flood	8. funny stuff
3. a hungry buffalo	6. double trouble	9. a loving mother

3 SOUNDS AND SPELLING

A. Listen to these word pairs. The first word has the [ə] vowel. If the vowel in the second word is the same, write *S*. If it is different, write *D*.

1. what, hat _D_	6. tough, though ____
2. flood, foot ____	7. cut, company ____
3. country, count ____	8. one, won ____
4. sun, son ____	9. done, bone ____
5. luck, lock ____	10. rush, touch ____

B. Work in small groups. Choose two pairs that are the same and two pairs that are different. Say them to your group.

4 SAYING SENTENCES

🎧 A. Listen to the lines of the poem and repeat them. In sentence 3, the *h* of *he* is not pronounced and *was he* is pronounced exactly like *Wuzzy*.

1. Fuzzy Wuzzy was a bear.

2. Fuzzy Wuzzy had no hair.

3. Fuzzy Wuzzy wasn't very fuzzy, was he?

 B. Practice the poem with a partner. Join words together and speak smoothly.

5 DIALOGUES

🎧 A. Listen and fill in the blanks. The missing words have the [ə] vowel.

Questions	Responses
1. What do you want for _____?	a. Not even _____ to take the _____.
2. Are you _____ than your _____?	b. She's _____ next _____.
3. How _____ _____ do you have?	c. No. He's the _____ _____ in the family.
4. Why did your _____ call?	d. _____. I'm not _____.
5. What happened to your _____?	e. I _____ it with a _____ knife.

 B. Work with a partner. Make five short dialogues by matching questions from the left column with responses from the right. Practice reading the dialogues.

[ə] CUP   23

6 LOVE AND MARRIAGE

 A. Listen to the words in the box and repeat them. The bold letters are pronounced [ə].

c**ou**ple	l**o**ve	come fr**o**m	each **o**ther	trust	cult**u**re

B. What is important for a successful marriage? Read the sentences below. Check the three statements that you think are most important for a successful marriage.

_____ 1. The couple should be in love.

_____ 2. The couple should trust each other.

_____ 3. The couple should like each other.

_____ 4. The couple should come from the same social class.

_____ 5. The couple should have the same religious beliefs.

_____ 6. The couple should have the same level of education.

_____ 7. The couple should come from the same culture.

_____ 8. The couple should have the same economic background.

_____ 9. The couple should be about the same age.

 C. Work in small groups. Compare your answers to Part B. Do you agree? Discuss your choices. What else is important in a successful marriage?

SELF-STUDY

🎧 **First listen to:**
- the phrases in Exercise 2.
- the word pairs in Exercise 3.

📼 **Now record them.**

Then record the sentences you checked in Exercise 6, Part B.

Tell why you think they are important.

UNIT 6 [ɑ] cop and [ə] cup

INTRODUCTION

Look at the pictures. They show you how to say the sounds [ɑ] and [ə].

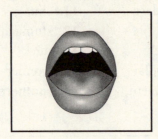 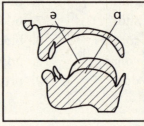 

[ɑ] cop, lock   [ə] cup, luck

Your mouth is very open.   Your mouth is almost closed.
Your tongue is low, in the   Your tongue is in the middle
center of your mouth.   of your mouth, neither high
                                  nor low.

Spellings for [ɑ]	Spellings for [ə]

Common
    o (between consonants):
    c**o**p, h**o**t, n**o**t, l**o**ck, p**o**ssible
Other
    a: w**a**nt, f**a**ther, w**a**tch, c**a**r, st**a**rt,
       h**a**rd, ch**a**rge
    ua: g**ua**rd
	See Unit 5.

FOCUSED PRACTICE

1 LISTEN AND PRACTICE: *Words with* [ɑ] *and* [ə]

🎧 Listen to these words and repeat them. Your mouth should be open for [ɑ].
Your mouth should be almost closed for [ə].

	[ɑ]				[ə]		
1.	rob	6.	modern	11.	shut	16.	tough
2.	shot	7.	odd	12.	stomach	17.	gun
3.	soccer	8.	block	13.	duck	18.	sudden
4.	collar	9.	popular	14.	wonder	19.	mustard
5.	dock	10.	problem	15.	southern	20.	hundred

2 VOWEL PATTERNS

🎧 A. Listen to these phrases and repeat them. The bold letters are the vowels
[ɑ] or [ə].

1. hot cup
2. double lock
3. lucky lottery winner
4. not enough
5. tough job
6. stop suddenly
7. modern country
8. hungry hogs
9. popular government
10. come on
11. hot summer
12. rotten luck
13. one block
14. young father

B. What is the vowel pattern of the phrases in Part A? Write each phrase in
the correct column.

[ɑ] [ə]	[ə] [ɑ]
hot cup	_____
_____	_____
_____	_____
_____	_____
_____	_____
_____	_____

C. Work with a partner. Check your lists in Part B and practice saying the phrases.

3 ██ **LISTEN FOR DIFFERENCES:** [ɑ] *versus* [ə]

🎧 **A.** Listen to these words and repeat them.

1. **a.** wants		5. **a.** collar		9. **a.** lock	
b. once		**b.** color		**b.** luck	
2. **a.** box		6. **a.** socks		10. **a.** cop	
b. bucks		**b.** sucks		**b.** cup	
3. **a.** shot		7. **a.** dock			
b. shut		**b.** duck			
4. **a.** rob		8. **a.** hot			
b. rub		**b.** hut			

🎧 **B.** Listen again and circle the words you hear.

4 ██ **BINGO:** *Words with* [ɑ] *and* [ə]

🎧 **A.** Listen to the words on the Bingo card and repeat them. Is your mouth open or almost closed? Write *open* under the words with [ɑ] and *closed* under the words with [ə].

1. lock *open*	6. once	11. hug	16. cop	21. collar	26. wants
2. socks	7. luck	12. not	17. bucks	22. robber	27. color
3. cut	8. shot	13. box	18. duck	23. shut	28. body
4. nut	9. rubber	14. buddy	19. hut	24. sucks	29. cot
5. hog	10. Don	15. cup	20. dock	25. done	30. hot

B. Now play Bingo. Use the card in Part A. Listen carefully and cross out each word you hear. When you have crossed out a complete row or column , say "Bingo!"

5 DIFFERENCES IN MEANING

Work with a partner and take turns. Read either question *a* or question *b* to your partner. Pronounce the last word carefully so your partner can read the correct response to you.

Questions	Responses
1. a. What's a dock?	A dock is a place where boats can tie up.
b. What's a duck?	A duck is a water bird that goes "quack-quack."
2. a. What's a cup?	A cup is a container for hot drinks.
b. What's a cop?	A cop is a police officer.
3. a. What's "succor"?	Succor is a formal word for "help."
b. What's soccer?	Soccer is the most popular sport in the world.
4. a. What's a knot?	You get a knot when you tie two strings together.
b. What's a nut?	A nut is a small food that is inside a shell.

6 IDIOMS AND EXPRESSIONS

A. Listen to these sentences and fill in the blanks.

1. We sold it all—_____, _____, and barrel.

2. The announcement sent _____ waves through the country.

3. We're in _____ _____ now.

4. Our new computer lab is _____ the _____ edge.

5. I only eat fast food _____ in a while.

6. This problem is going to be a _____ _____ to crack.

B. **Work with a partner. Check your answers for Part A. Then match the idioms in the shaded boxes with one of the definitions below. Practice saying the sentences in Part A.**

    a. shocked

    b. occasionally

    c. everything

    d. very modern and up-to-date

    e. in trouble

    f. difficult to solve

    🎧 **First listen to:**

- the words in Exercise 1.

- the phrases in Exercise 2.

    📼 **Now record them.**

Then make up a short story about a cop and robber and record it.

Try to include some of the following [ɑ] and [ə] words.

[ɑ]	[ə]
cop	(hand)cuffs
drop	luck, lucky, unlucky
problem	money
rob, robber, robbery	suddenly
stop	trouble

Review: [ɛ] net, [æ] Nat, [ə] nut, and [ɑ] not

FOCUSED PRACTICE

> **1** **LISTEN AND PRACTICE:** *Words with* [ɛ], [æ], [ə], *and* [ɑ]

🎧 **A.** Listen to the words in each row and repeat them. Use the diagrams to help you pronounce the vowels correctly.

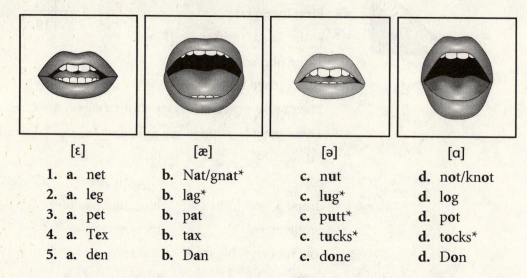

[ɛ]	[æ]	[ə]	[ɑ]
1. a. net	**b.** Nat/gnat*	**c.** nut	**d.** not/knot
2. a. leg	**b.** lag*	**c.** lug*	**d.** log
3. a. pet	**b.** pat	**c.** putt*	**d.** pot
4. a. Tex	**b.** tax	**c.** tucks*	**d.** tocks*
5. a. den	**b.** Dan	**c.** done	**d.** Don

gnat: small flying insect; *lag:* follow behind; *lug:* carry; *putt:* short golf shot; *tucks:* folds; *tocks:* part of a clock sound—clocks go "tick tock"

 B. Work with a partner. Take turns saying one of the words in Part A. Your partner will tell you which word you said.

2   BINGO: *Words with* [ɛ], [æ], [ə], *and* [ɑ]

A. Listen to the words on the Bingo card and repeat them. Write [ɛ], [æ], [ə], or [ɑ] under each word.

1. lock *[ɑ]*	6. blonder	11. guest	16. collar
2. blender	7. Don	12. blander*	17. gust*
3. color	8. lack	13. Keller	18. hum
4. wants	9. gassed	14. ham	19. luck
5. hem*	10. blunder*	15. done	20. once

*hem: bottom edge of clothing, turned under to form a clean edge; *blunder:* mistake; *blander:* comparative of *bland,* without much taste; *gust:* burst of wind

B. Now play Bingo. Use the card in Part A. Listen carefully and cross out each word you hear. When you have crossed out a complete row or column ⊞ ⊞ , say "Bingo!"

3   SAYING SENTENCES

A. Listen to these sentences and repeat them. When you say a sentence, group words into phrases and speak smoothly. The underlined words in the first sentence show one way to group the words in that sentence.

1. The peppy puppy ate the poppies.

2. Are Dan and Don done in the den?

3. Nat did not put the nuts in the net.

4. The big black bug bled black blood.

B. Work in small groups. Take turns reading a sentence to the group.

4 DIFFERENCES IN MEANING

Work with a partner and take turns. Read either sentence *a* or sentence *b* to your partner. Pronounce the underlined word carefully so your partner can read the correct response to you.

Sentences   **Responses**

1. **a.** Watch out! There's a <u>bog</u> over there!   I've got my boots on.

   b. Watch out! There's a <u>bug</u> over there!   I'm not afraid of insects.

2. **a.** Isn't that a <u>gnat</u> in your soup?   How disgusting! Waiter, take this back!

   b. Isn't that a <u>nut</u> in your soup?   Yes, it's made with peanuts.

3. **a.** What kind of <u>luck</u> do you have?   None—I've never won anything in my life.

   b. What kind of <u>lock</u> do you have?   A really strong one—I'm afraid of burglars.

4. **a.** They made a lot of noise when they <u>left</u>.   Even the neighbors heard the banging doors.

   b. They made a lot of noise when they <u>laughed</u>.   The movie was really funny.

5 DIALOGUE

A. Listen to this dialogue and repeat the lines. Follow the intonation lines (showing how your voice rises or falls) when you say the question words. Grandma's voice rises on the question when she doesn't hear what Pat said. Her voice falls on the question when she wants more information.

Pat: Hi, Grandma. I've got some news.

Grandma: Oh, hi, Pat. What did you say?

Pat: I have some news to tell you, Grandma.

Grandma: What, dear?

Pat: My company's sending me to Europe.

Grandma: Where?

Pat: Europe, Grandma. My company's sending me to Europe.

Grandma: Oh, that's nice, Pat. Where?

Pat: To France, to Paris. I'm leaving next week.

Grandma: Oh, so soon? When?

Pat: Next Saturday. I want to come to see you tomorrow.

Grandma: Yes, please come. I'm going to miss you, Pat.

Pat: I'll miss you too, Grandma. But I'll only be there for two months.

B. Work with a partner. Practice the dialogue in Part A.

6 DIALOGUES

A. Work with a partner. Practice the dialogues below. Follow the intonation lines.

1. **A:** I have something to tell you.

   B: What?

   A: I said I have something to tell you.

2. **A:** I have something to tell you.

   B: What?

   A: I got a promotion!

B. Complete the dialogues below. When you read B's part, use rising intonation with the question word to show you didn't hear or use falling intonation with the question word to show you want more information.

1. **A:** I have some bad news.

   B: What?

   A: _____

2. **A:** There's a dance this weekend.

   B: When?

   A: _____

🎧 **First listen to:**

- the words in Exercises 1 and 2.
- the sentences in Exercise 3.

📼 **Now record them.**

UNIT 8 [r] after vowels

INTRODUCTION

Look at the diagram and pictures. They show you how to say the sounds [ər], [or], and [ɑr].

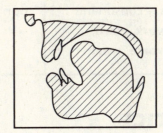

To make [r] after a vowel, turn the tip of your tongue up and back.

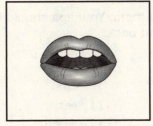

[ər] her, hurt

Your lips are almost closed.
The tip of your tongue turns up and back.

[or] more, four

Your lips are rounded.
The tip of your tongue turns up and back.

[ɑr] heart, car

Your mouth is very open.
The tip of your tongue turns up and back.

- In most dialects of American English, [r] is pronounced after vowels.
- In some words, an unstressed *e* before *r* is not pronounced. These words look as if *e* should be a syllable, but most English speakers do not pronounce it:

every: say "evry"   interest: say "intrəst"   general: say "genrəl"

several: say "sevrəl"   temperature: say "temprətʃər"   different: say "diffrənt"

Spellings for [ər]	Spellings for [or]	Spellings for [ɑr]

Common
ir: **b**ir**d**, **c**ir**cle**, **f**ir**st**
ur: **t**ur**n**, **b**ur**n**, **h**ur**t**
er: **h**er, **s**er**ve**, **w**er**e**
Other
ear: **h**ear**d**, **ear**th,
    early
wor + consonant:
    work, **wor**d,
    worse, **wor**th
	Common
	or: **for**, **m**or**e**, **sh**or**t**
	
	Other
	war: **war**, **war**m, **war**n
	our: **f**our
	oor: **fl**oor
		Common
		ar: **ar**e, **c**ar, **h**ar**d**
		
		Other
		ear: **h**ear**t**
		uar: **g**uar**d**

FOCUSED PRACTICE

1   LISTEN AND PRACTICE: *Words with* [ər]

🎧 A. Listen to these words and repeat them. Your lips should be almost closed. Turn the tip of your tongue up and back.

1. bird	5. turn	9. worse	13. her
2. burn	6. heard	10. first	14. were
3. word	7. hurt	11. serve	15. shirt
4. circle	8. work	12. earth	16. term

👥 B. Work in small groups. Take turns saying four words to the group.

2   LISTEN AND PRACTICE: *Words with* [or]

🎧 A. Listen to these words and repeat them. Round your lips. Turn the tip of your tongue up and back.

1. tore	5. more	9. door
2. sore	6. short	10. warm
3. war	7. corn	11. four
4. shore	8. formal	12. floor

👥 B. Work in small groups. Take turns saying four words to the group.

3 LISTEN AND PRACTICE: *Words with* [ɑr]

🎧 A. Listen to these words and repeat them. Your mouth should be open. Turn the tip of your tongue up and back.

1. car	5. heart	9. part
2. start	6. large	10. garden
3. yard	7. charge	11. guard
4. hard	8. sharp	12. mark

👥 B. Work in small groups. Take turns saying four words to the group.

4 SOUNDS AND SPELLING

🎧 A. Listen to these word pairs. If the bold sounds are the same, write *S*. If the bold sounds are different, write *D*.

1. here, hear _S_

2. were, war ___

3. perfect, pardon ___

4. work, word ___

5. burn, bird ___

6. war, wore ___

7. her, hair ___

8. heard, hard ___

9. hurt, word ___

10. worse, wore ___

11. heard, beard ___

12. worm, warm ___

👥 B. Work in small groups. Choose two pairs that are the same and two pairs that are different. Say them to the group.

5 LISTEN FOR DIFFERENCES: [ər] *versus* [ɔr] *versus* [ɑr]

🎧 A. Listen to these words and repeat them.

1. word	4. war	7. heard	10. heart
2. hard	5. warn	8. large	11. born
3. work	6. her	9. horn	12. guard

B. Look at the words in Part A. Write each word in the correct column.

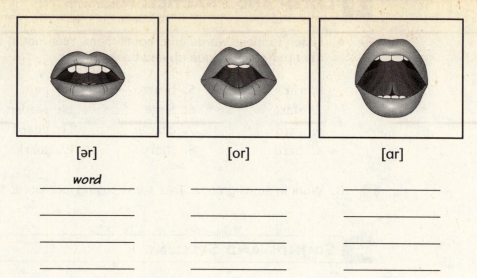

[ər]	[or]	[ɑr]
word		
_____	_____	_____
_____	_____	_____
_____	_____	_____

 C. Work with a partner. Check your lists. Practice saying the words in each column. Use the diagrams to help you pronounce the words.

6 GAME: *Vowels + r*

 Play this game in two teams—Team 1 and Team 2. Score points for correct answers, correctly pronounced.

Team 1: Ask the questions on page 191 to the players on Team 2.

Team 2: Answer the questions with a word that has the [ər], [or], or [ɑr] vowel. Then ask Team 1 the questions on page 194.

EXAMPLE

Team 1:	What's 3 +1?
Team 2:	*Four.*
Team 2:	What's the opposite of *tall?*
Team 1:	*Short.*

A. Read the skills in the chart below. Add a skill at the end of the chart. Check the things you know how to do.

Do you know how to . . . ?	You	Student 1	Student 2
1. ride a bike			
2. play (a musical instrument)			
3. play (a sport)			
4. swim			
5. drive a car			
6. type with all ten fingers			
7. _____			

B. Work in groups of three. Ask the other members of your group which skills they have. Complete the chart in Part A.

C. Discuss learning new skills with your group. Use these questions as models:

- Do you remember how/when you learned to . . . ?
- Did you learn to . . . quickly and easily?
- Was it hard to learn to . . . ?

SELF-STUDY

🎧 **First listen to:**
- the words in Exercises 1, 2, and 3.

▣▣ **Now record them.**

Then make a one-minute recording about your experience learning English or learning one of the skills in Exercise 7. Use some of these words in your recording:

- hard, first, embarrassed, learn, discouraged, understand, tired, determined, work, worry, important, better, nervous

UNIT 9 [ow] boat, [ɑ] pot, and [ɔ] bought

INTRODUCTION

Look at the pictures. They show you how to say the sounds [ow], [ɑ], and [ɔ].

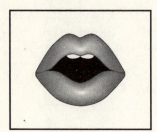

[ow] boat, go

Round your lips.
End [ow] in a [w] sound.

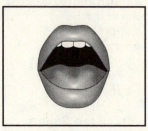

[ɑ] pot, father

Open your mouth.
Don't round your lips.
Pronounce the vowel in
the center of your mouth.

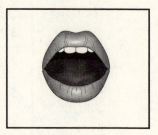

[ɔ] bought, caught

Open your mouth and
round your lips a little.

• When another vowel follows [ow], join the two vowels with [w].

go^win   show_up

Spellings for [ow]	Spellings for [ɑ]	Spellings for [ɔ]

Common
  o: **go**, **no**, he**llo**, m**ost**,
    told
  oCe (C is a consonant;
    e is silent): r**ode**, th**ose**,
    j**oke**, n**ose**, h**ome**
  oa: b**oat**, c**oat**, r**oad**
  ow: kn**ow**, sh**ow**, wind**ow**
Other
  oe: t**oe**, **Joe**
  ough: th**ough**, d**ough**
  ew: s**ew**
	See Unit 6.	Common
		  o + *n* or *s*: l**ong**, b**oss**,
		             l**ost**, wr**ong**,
		             a**cross**
		  au: c**aught**, **August**,
		    audience
		  aw: fl**aw**, dr**aw**, l**aw**,
		    awful
		  al: t**all**, s**alt**, **also**, **all**, f**all**
		Other
		  ough: th**ought**, **ough**t
		  oa: br**oad**

FOCUSED PRACTICE

1 LISTEN AND PRACTICE: *Words with* [ow], [ɑ], *and* [ɔ]

🎧 Listen to these words and repeat them.

[ow]		[ɑ]		[ɔ]	
1. coat		8. rob		15. fought	
2. frozen		9. shot		16. thought	
3. October		10. cop		17. long	
4. show		11. rock		18. loss	
5. drove		12. stocking		19. caught	
6. ago		13. car		20. law	
7. home		14. possible		21. crawl	

2 DIALECT DIFFERENCES: [ɑ] *versus* [ɔ]

• Many Americans from the Midwest and West do not use the vowel [ɔ]. They pronounce words like *bought* and *loss* with [ɑ], the vowel in *pot* and *father*. Many Americans from the Northeast use both the [ɑ] and [ɔ] vowels.

🎧 A. Listen to these words. You will hear each word twice. The first speaker is from Seattle, Washington. This speaker uses the vowel [ɑ]. The second speaker is from New York. The New Yorker uses the vowel [ɔ]. Can you hear the difference in the vowels of the two speakers?

	Seattle [ɑ]	New York [ɔ]
1. fault		
2. bought		
3. loss		
4. thought		
5. taught		
6. long		
7. boss		
8. draw		

🎧 B. Listen again. You will hear each word in Part A once. Is the speaker from Seattle or New York? If you hear [ɑ], check the *Seattle* column. If you hear [ɔ], check the *New York* column.

3 LISTEN FOR DIFFERENCES

🎧 A. Listen to these words and repeat them.

1. a. wrote	4. a. clothes	7. a. bold
b. rot	b. claws	b. bald
2. a. loan	5. a. score	8. a. coat
b. lawn	b. scar	b. cot
3. a. scold	6. a. comb	9. a. boat
b. scald	b. calm	b. bought

🎧 B. Listen again and circle the words you hear.

4 DIFFERENCES IN MEANING

  Work with a partner and take turns. Read either sentence *a* or sentence *b* to your partner. Pronounce the vowels carefully so your partner can read the correct response to you.

Sentences

1. a. What do you think of this c**oa**t?

   b. What do you think of this c**o**t?

2. a. Do you think he was c**o**ld?

   b. Do you think he was c**a**lled?

3. a. What happened? That's a horrible sc**a**r!

   b. What happened? That's a horrible sc**o**re!

4. a. I really need a l**aw**n.
   b. I really need a l**oa**n.

Responses

It fits you perfectly!

I'd rather have a real bed!

Yes. His lips were blue, and his teeth were chattering.

Yes. Nancy said she spoke to him last night.

I cut myself.

I didn't study.

Why don't you plant some grass?
Why don't you go to the bank?

5 LISTENING: *What does "home" mean?*

🎧 A. Listen to the three views of "home." Take notes as you listen.

Sanctuary*	Gathering Place	Pit Stop*

*A *sanctuary* is a safe place. A *pit stop* is a very quick stop that race-car drivers make to change tires, get gas, etc.

  B. Work in groups of three. Explain the three speakers' views of their homes.

6 INTERVIEWS: *Tell me about your home.*

A. Read the questions in the chart below and write short answers in the *You* column.

	You	Student 1	Student 2
1. Where are you living now? (house, apartment, dormitory, etc.)			
2. Who do you live with?			
3. How do you feel if people drop by and visit without calling first?			
4. When you have free time, would you rather stay home or go out?			
5. Do you like to entertain at home?			

continued

[OW] BOAT, [ɑ] POT, AND [ɔ] BOUGHT   43

	You	Student 1	Student 2
6. Do you think "home" should be a sanctuary, a gathering place, or a pit stop? Which is your home like now?			
7. What was your home like when you were a child?			

 B. Work in groups of three. Ask the other members of your group the questions and complete the chart in Part A.

🎧 **First listen to:**

- the words in Exercises 1 and 3.

📼 **Now record them.**

Then make a short recording describing your home and what you do there. Is your home more like a sanctuary, a gathering place, or a pit stop?

UNIT 10 [uw] f<u>oo</u>d and [ʊ] b<u>oo</u>k

INTRODUCTION

Look at the pictures. They show you how to say the sounds [uw] and [ʊ].

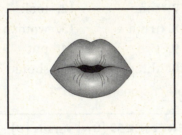

[uw] f<u>oo</u>d, d<u>o</u>   [ʊ] b<u>oo</u>k, c<u>ou</u>ld

Round your lips tightly.   Your lips are less rounded
End [uw] in a [w] sound.   for [ʊ] than for [uw].

- When another vowel follows [uw], join the two vowels with [w].

    Do⁀ʷit   Who⁀ʷis it?

Spellings for [uw]	Spellings for [ʊ]
Common oo: **food, cool, noon, choose** u: **student, rude, truth, revolution** **Other** **do, who, move, group, through** **new, grew, suit, juice, beauty**	**Common** oo: **good, foot, look, hood** u: **put, pull, sugar, push** **Other** **would, could, should, woman**

FOCUSED PRACTICE

1 | LISTEN AND PRACTICE: *Words with* [uw] *and* [ʊ]

🎧 Listen to these words and repeat them.

	[uw]			[ʊ]
1. June	6. blue	11. book	16. could
2. include	7. soon	12. look	17. cook
3. introduce	8. truth	13. woman	18. sugar
4. fool	9. two	14. put	19. hood
5. move	10. threw	15. should	20. wool

2 | LISTEN FOR DIFFERENCES: [uw] *versus* [ʊ]

🎧 A. Listen to these words and repeat them.

1. a. Luke	3. a. cooed*	5. a. who'd	7. a. stewed*
b. look	b. could	b. hood	b. stood
2. a. suit	4. a. shooed*	6. a. pool	8. a. fool
b. soot*	b. should	b. pull	b. full

*soot: black ash; coo: make a low soft sound; shoo: wave someone away; stew: slowly cook meat and vegetables

🎧 B. Listen again and circle the words you hear.

3 | RHYMES

🎧 A. Listen to the poem and repeat the lines. Group words together.

How much wood would a woodchuck* chuck*

If a woodchuck could chuck wood?

Just as much as a woodchuck would

If a woodchuck could chuck wood.

*woodchuck: a beaver-sized animal that tunnels in the ground; chuck: throw (slang)

B. Now practice the poem with a partner.

---

4   IDIOMS AND EXPRESSIONS WITH [uw] AND [ʊ]

A. Listen to the phrases in column A and repeat them. The bold vowels are [uw] or [ʊ].

A   **B**

1. ___ bl**a**ck and bl**ue**   a. please yourself

2. ___ p**u**ll something off   b. an opportunity to enter something

3. ___ s**ui**t yourself   c. bruised

4. ___ tr**ue** to form   d. fight ferociously

5. ___ p**u**t up with   e. endure, tolerate

6. ___ f**oo**d for thought   f. following a pattern

7. ___ (have) a f**oo**t in the door g. something to think about

8. ___ fight t**oo**th and nail   h. do something in spite of difficulties

B. Match each phrase in column A with its definition in column B. Then check your answers with your partner.

C. Work in small groups. Take turns asking for and giving definitions of the idioms in Part A. Use complete sentences.

EXAMPLE

What does "black and blue" mean?

"Black and blue" means "bruised."

---

5   DIALOGUES

A. Work with a partner. Complete the dialogues with idioms from Exercise 4.

1. **A:** Was June hurt badly in the accident?
   B: No. She was _____ _____ _____ all over, but she didn't have any broken bones.

2. A: Your roommate is so messy! How do you stand it?

B: He lets me use his car, and I _____ _____

_____ his mess.

3. A: Do you really think I can get a job with the newspaper?

B: Well, I'd say you already have _____ _____

_____ _____ _____—you're dating the

editor's daughter!

4. A: I know you don't approve, but I'm going to buy that sports car!

B: Okay—_____ _____. But don't forget—you

have to pay for the gas!

B. Work with a partner. Practice the dialogues in Part A.

---

6 DILEMMAS: could, should, *and* would

A. A "dilemma" is a problem that doesn't have an easy solution. Read Max's
dilemmas. Then write three solutions. Use *could* to describe possible things
Max could do. Use *should* to give advice to Max. Use *would* to say what
you would do in the same situation.

1. Max sees his best friend's wife kissing another man.

What could Max do? _____

What should Max do? _____

What would you do in this situation? _____

2. Max's classmate June asks Max if she can copy his homework.

What could Max do? _____

What should Max do? _____

What would you do in this situation? _____

3. The cashier in the restaurant gave Max an extra ten dollars in change.

What could Max do? _____

What should Max do? _____

What would you do in this situation? _____

4. While Max was parking his car, he hit the car behind him and broke the other car's headlight.

What could Max do? _____

What should Max do? _____

What would you do in this situation? _____

 B. Work in small groups. Discuss your solutions to Max's dilemmas.

SELF-STUDY

🎧 **First listen to:**

• the words in Exercises 1 and 2.

📼 **Now record them.**

Then record a one-minute description of a dilemma from Exercise 6 (or use one that you are facing). Describe the dilemma and some possible solutions, using *could* or *should*. Use *would* to describe what you would do.

CONSONANTS

INTRODUCTION

🎧 • There are twenty-four consonants in English. Listen to these words.

pie [p]	**p**res**s**ure [ʃ]
buy [b]	plea**s**ure [ʒ]
tie [t]	**ch**ain [tʃ]
die [d]	**J**ane [dʒ]
came [k]	**r**ight [r]
game [g]	**l**ight [l]
fairy [f]	**s**ome [m]
very [v]	**s**u**n** [n]
thin [θ]	su**ng** [ŋ]
then [ð]	**y**es [y]
Sue [s]	**w**et [w]
zoo [z]	**h**ead [h]

CONSONANTS ARE MADE

Many consonants are made by moving the tongue close to or touching some part of the mouth.

I	**THE MOUTH**

Look at the drawing of the mouth and its parts. Label the parts of the mouth. Use the words in the box.

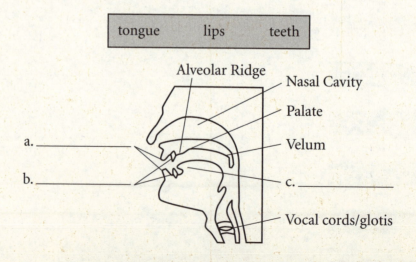

tongue	lips	teeth

Alveolar Ridge

Nasal Cavity

Palate

Velum

a. _____

b. _____

c. _____

Vocal cords/glotis

2 CONSONANTS MADE WITH THE LIPS

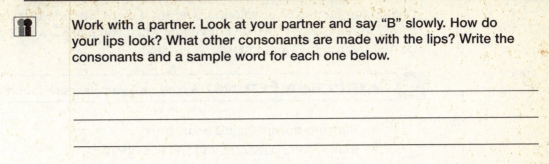

Work with a partner. Look at your partner and say "B" slowly. How do your lips look? What other consonants are made with the lips? Write the consonants and a sample word for each one below.

_____

_____

_____

_____

3 OTHER CONSONANTS

A. First look at the mouth diagrams and their consonants.

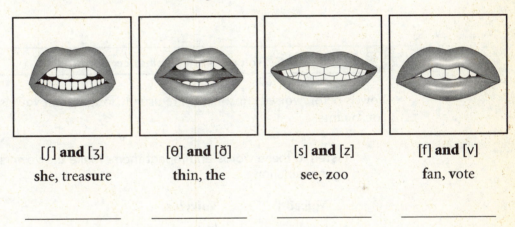

| [ʃ] **and** [ʒ] | [θ] **and** [ð] | [s] **and** [z] | [f] **and** [v] |
| she, treasure | thin, the | see, zoo | fan, vote |

_____   _____   _____   _____

_____   _____   _____   _____

B. Work with a partner. Take turns facing each other and saying the words in the box slowly. Exaggerate the bold sound in each word. Your partner will look at your lips as you say the bold sound and write the word under the most similar diagram.

| kiss | with | laugh | wash | bees | both | five | measure |

VOICED AND VOICELESS CONSONANTS

Consonants are voiced or voiceless. The vocal cords vibrate when you make a voiced sound like [z]. They do not vibrate when you make a voiceless sound like [s]. You can feel the vibration with your hand.

| **4** | **SAYING AND FEELING:** *Voiced and voiceless consonants* |

a. Put your fingers against your throat.
b. Make a long [zzzzzzz], and feel the vibration.
c. Make a long [sssssss]. What do you feel?
d. Switch back and forth between the two sounds:
   [zzzzz-ssssss-zzzzzz-ssssssss]
e. Repeat steps *a* to *c*, using [vvvvv] and [fffff].
   Is [v] voiced or voiceless? Is [f] voiced or voiceless?

| **5** | **LISTENING:** *Voiced and voiceless consonants* |

Vowels before voiced consonants are usually longer than vowels before voiceless consonants.

A. Listen to these words and repeat them. Make the vowels before voiced consonants long.

Voiced	**Voiceless**
1. leave	leaf
2. peas	peace
3. razor	racer
4. edge	etch
5. pig	pick
6. robe	rope
7. ride	write
8. prize	price

B. Listen again and circle the words you hear.

6 FILL IN THE GRID

 Work with a partner. Each of you has a grid that is partially filled in with words. Student A has the words that are missing from Student B's grid, and Student B has the words that are missing from Student A's grid. Don't show your grid to your partner. Take turns asking each other for missing words. After you are done, compare your grids. They should be the same. Students A's grid is on page 191. Student B's grid is on page 194.

STOP CONSONANTS AND CONTINUANTS

The stop consonants are [p], [b], [t], [d], [k], and [g]. When you say a stop consonant, the air is completely stopped for a moment.

All other English consonants are continuants. When you say a continuant, the air is not stopped. When you want someone to be quiet, you say "Shhhhh," a long continuant.

7 STOPS OR CONTINUANTS?

🎧 A. Listen to the final sounds in these words. Circle the words that end in continuants.

1. egg	5. rob	9. please
2. cash	6. choose	10. stop
3. hard	7. salt	11. love
4. month	8. car	12. like

 B. Work with a partner. Practice saying the words to each other.

A. When [p], [t], or [k] begin a word and are followed by a stressed vowel, they are pronounced with aspiration, a strong puff of air. Listen to these words and repeat them. Pronounce the first consonant with a strong puff of air (written " ʿ ").

1. pʿie	4. tʿea	7. kʿill
2. pʿiece	5. tʿwo	8. cʿar
3. pʿay	6. tʿime	9. cʿool

B. Work with a partner. Take a piece of paper. Hold it so the bottom edge is about 2 inches (5 centimeters) from your lips. Say the words from the first column (the [p] words) to your partner. When you say the words, the aspiration should blow the paper away from your lips. Your partner will see whether the paper moves.

JOINING FINAL CONSONANTS TO THE NEXT WORD

The pronunciation of final consonants depends on the sound that follows.

- Final Consonant + Vowel: *stand‿up*

  Final consonants join clearly to words beginning with vowels.

- Final Consonant + Same Consonant: *half͡full*

  When a word ends in a consonant and the next word begins with the same consonant, say one long consonant (written "͡"). Don't say the consonant twice.

- Final Consonant + Different Consonant: *blackʾ bag*

  When a word ends in a consonant and the next word begins with a different consonant, keep the final consonant short (written "ʾ"). Hold the final consonant until you say the next word.

9 JOINING SOUNDS

🎧 Listen to these phrases and repeat them. Join words together.

1. stand up
2. ask Anna
3. main entrance
4. home address

5. both things
6. black car
7. car radio
8. wet towel

9. watch TV
10. big dinner
11. lose time
12. job description

10 DIALOGUES

🎧 A. Listen to the sentences in columns A and B. Write the words you hear in the blanks.

A	B
1. What's your _____ _____?	a. It's _____ _____. I hung _____ _____.
2. Please don't leave your _____ _____ on the floor.	b. How about a nice _____ _____?
3. Let's meet at the _____ _____ at ten o'clock.	c. Five thirty five _____ _____.
4. The _____ _____ isn't working.	d. Yeah. It's too _____ _____ go to a movie.
5. I'm really hungry. Let's have a _____ _____.	e. OK, but let's _____ _____ 10:15.
6. Shall we _____ _____ tonight?	f. I know. But it's too expensive to _____ _____.

👥 B. Work with a partner. Create short dialogues by matching a sentence from column A and a response from column B. Practice the dialogues.

UNIT 12 Beginning and final consonants

INTRODUCTION

Beginning Voiceless Stop Consonants: [p], [t], and [k]

- Pronounce [p], [t], and [k] with aspiration (a strong puff of air) when they begin a word and are followed by a stressed vowel.

  p'an   t'oo   c'ome

  pan

- Pronounce [p], [t], and [k] with aspiration when they begin a stressed syllable.

  rep'eat   ret'urn   ac'ademy

Joining Final Consonants to the Next Word

- Final Consonant + Vowel: *fresh air*

  Join the consonant and vowel clearly.

  stop it   read a book

- Final Stop Consonant + Same Stop Consonant: *black car*

  Hold the final stop consonant ([p], [b], [t], [d], [k], [g]). Release it when you say the next word. Don't say the consonant twice.

  What time?   stop playing   black coat

- Final Consonant + Same Consonant: *half full*

  Say one long consonant. Don't say the consonant twice.

  ten names   raise zebras   wash shirts

- Final Consonant + Different Consonant: *good people*

  Say the final consonant, but keep it short. Say the next word immediately. Don't release the final consonant strongly. Don't separate the two consonants with a vowel sound.

  big dinner   stop talking   five dollars

Vowels before Final Voiced and Voiceless Consonants: *made, make*

- Vowels before voiced consonants are longer than vowels before voiceless consonants.

  Longer vowels: made laid prove rise

  Shorter vowels: make late proof rice

FOCUSED PRACTICE

1 ASPIRATION

A. Listen to these words and repeat them. Aspirate the beginning consonant.

1. p⁽ill	6. t⁽ell	11. k⁽ey
2. p⁽en	7. T⁽om	12. c⁽ow
3. p⁽eas	8. t⁽our	13. c⁽ame
4. ap⁽art	9. att⁽end	14. occ⁽ur
5. dep⁽end	10. ret⁽ire	15. acc⁽ount

B. The consonants [p], [t], and [k] are aspirated only before stressed vowels. Listen to these words. Place a stress mark (′) over the stressed vowel. Is the bold consonant aspirated or not? Write *A* in the blank if the bold consonant is aspirated. Write *U* if it is not aspirated.

1. ápples _____U_____   4. attack _____

2. appear _____   5. accomplish _____

3. today _____   6. bacon _____

C. Check your answers with a partner and practice saying the words from Part B.

2 JOINING FINAL CONSONANTS

A. Listen to these phrases and repeat them.

Final Consonant + Vowel	**Final Consonant + Same Consonant**
1. Miss Anderson	Miss Sanderson
2. keep ants	keep pants
3. wrote "L"	wrote "tell"
4. take oats*	take coats
5. kiss Andy	kiss Sandy
6. love Ann	love Van
7. hug* us	hug Gus
8. chase Ally	chase Sally

oats: a grain or cereal; *hug:* put your arms around someone

B. Listen again and circle the phrases you hear.

C. Work with a partner. Take turns reading a phrase from Part A and pointing to the phrase you hear.

D. Now listen to these sentences. Fill in the blanks with phrases from Part A. Practice saying the sentences.

1. Did you invite _____ or _____?

2. _____ inside; _____ outside.

3. You _____, and I _____.

4. _____ to the cleaners; _____ to the horses.

5. You _____, and I'll _____.

6. I _____, and you _____.

7. If you _____, you should also _____.

8. You _____, and I'll _____.

3 LISTEN FOR DIFFERENCES: *Voiced versus voiceless consonants*

A. Listen to these words and repeat them. The vowels in the *a* words precede voiced consonants. The vowels in the *b* words precede voiceless consonants. Make the vowels in the *a* words longer than the vowels in the *b* words.

1. a. had		4. a. seed		7. a. dug	
b. hat		b. seat		b. duck	
2. a. cab		5. a. stayed		8. a. pig	
b. cap		b. state		b. pick	
3. a. robe		6. a. said		9. a. log	
b. rope		b. set		b. lock	

B. Listen again and circle the words you hear.

4 FINAL CONSONANTS AND COMPOUND NOUNS

🎧 **A.** Listen to these compound nouns and repeat them. Say the first word with heavy stress (´) and high pitch (a high note). Say the second word with lighter stress (`) and low pitch.

1. stóp sìgn
2. jób àd
3. lánguage còurse
4. fárm ànimals
5. góld mìne
6. jób tràining
7. trável àgent
8. lóve trìangle
9. ólive òil
10. júnk màil
11. bíke pàth
12. árt exhìbit

🎧 **B.** Listen to the compounds again. How do the final consonants join to the next noun? If the next noun begins with a vowel, underline the joining. If the next noun begins with a different consonant, mark the final consonant to show that it is not released (`).

 C. Check your answers with a partner. Practice saying the compound nouns.

5 DEFINITIONS

 A. Work with a partner. Make sure you know what the compound nouns in Exercise 4 mean. Then take turns asking for and giving definitions of the compound nouns in Exercise 4. Use complete sentences.

EXAMPLE

What's a "language course"?

A "language course" is a class you take to learn a language.

🎧 **First listen to:**

- the words in Exercise 1.
- the phrases in Exercise 2.

📼 **Now record them.**

Then record the definitions of the compound nouns in Exercise 4.

Use complete sentences.

INTRODUCTION

The regular past tense -*ed* ending has three pronunciations: [t], [d], and [əd] (or [ɪd]). The pronunciation depends on the last sound of the base verb.

For verbs ending in . . .	pronounce the -*ed* ending . . .	Examples
[t] or [d]	as a new syllable: [əd] or [ɪd]	visit—visit**ed** [təd]
		land—land**ed** [dəd]
a voiceless sound: [p, k, θ, f, s, ʃ, tʃ]	as a final sound: [t]	like—lik**ed** [kt]
		kiss—kiss**ed** [st]
a voiced sound: [b, g, ð, v, z, ʒ, dʒ, m, n, ŋ, r, l] or a vowel	as a final sound: [d]	love—lov**ed** [vd]
		stay—st**ayed** [eyd]

FOCUSED PRACTICE

I **LISTEN AND PRACTICE:** *Hearing syllables*

🎧 A. Listen to these present and past tense verbs, and repeat them.

1. a. repeat _2_
    b. repeated _3_

2. a. decide ___
    b. decided ___

3. a. investigate ___
    b. investigated ___

4. a. end ___
    b. ended ___

5. a. create ___
    b. created ___

6. a. paint ___
    b. painted ___

7. a. expect ___
    b. expected ___

8. a. add ___
    b. added ___

B. Underline the syllables in the verbs in Part A. Then write the number of syllables.

C. Review the rule. Complete these sentences.

1. All of the present tense verbs in Part A end in a _____ or _____ sound.

2. The past tense ending is pronounced as a new _____.

---

2 LISTEN AND PRACTICE: *Hearing endings*

A. Listen to these present and past tense verbs, and repeat them.

1. **a.** stop
   b. stopped _[t]_

2. **a.** call
   b. called ___

3. **a.** reach
   b. reached ___

4. **a.** hug
   b. hugged ___

5. **a.** ask
   b. asked ___

6. **a.** believe
   b. believed ___

7. **a.** dream
   b. dreamed ___

8. **a.** continue
   b. continued ___

B. What is the sound of the past tense ending of the verbs in Part A? Write [t] or [d] in the blanks.

C. Review the rule. Circle the correct answer.

The past tense ending of the verbs in Part A (is / is not) pronounced as an extra syllable.

---

3 APPLY THE RULE: *Past tense endings*

A. Work with a partner. How is the past tense of these verbs pronounced? Write [əd], [t], or [d] after each verb to show how it is pronounced.

1. want _____[əd]_____

2. enjoy _____

3. vote _____

4. wash _____

5. demand _____

6. help _____

7. study _____

8. clean _____

B. Work with a partner. Take turns saying the present and past tense of the verbs in Part A.

4 GAME: *Past tense endings*

 Play this game in two teams—Team 1 and Team 2. Give points for correct answers, correctly pronounced.

Team 1: Read the verbs on page 191 to the players on Team 2.

Team 2: Answer with the past tense of the verbs. Then read Team 1 the verbs on page 194.

> ### EXAMPLE
>
> **Team 1:** call
>
> **Team 2:** *called*

5 DIALOGUES

A. Listen to the phrases in the box and repeat them. Join final consonants and beginning vowels.

> | | | |
> |---|---|---|
> | watched a while | started over | looked at three |
> | seemed angry | ordered it | waited all day |

B. Work with a partner. Complete the dialogues, using the phrases from the box. Then practice the dialogues.

1. **A:** Did you see the game?

   B: I _____, but then I fell asleep.

2. **A:** Did you find a new apartment?

   B: No. I _____ apartments, but they were all too small.

3. **A:** Are you still working on that essay?

   B: Yes. I didn't like what I'd written, so I _____.

4. **A:** Did you find the book you need?

   B: Not at the bookstore, but I _____ on the Internet.

5. **A:** Did the cable repairman come?

   B: No. I _____, but he never showed up.

6. **A:** How are you?

   B: I'm fine. How are you? You _____ this morning.

6 LISTEN FOR DIFFERENCES: *Present versus past tense*

A. Listen to these dialogues and repeat them. Circle the verbs you hear. Then write *do* or *did* in the blanks.

1. **Lucy:** I (need/needed) some money.

   Sylvia: So _____ I.

2. **Lucy:** I (travel/traveled) a lot.

   Sylvia: So _____ I.

3. **Lucy:** I (work/worked) so hard.

   Sylvia: So _____ I.

4. **Lucy:** I (help/helped) Mom and Dad a lot.

   Sylvia: So _____ I.

5. **Lucy:** I (clean/cleaned) on Saturday.

   Sylvia: So _____ I.

B. Work with a partner. Practice the dialogues in Part A. When you say Lucy's part, choose the present or the past tense. Pronounce the verb correctly. Your partner will decide whether to answer with "do" or "did." Take turns saying Lucy's and Sylvia's parts.

7 LISTENING: *"Not a Perfect Crime"*

A. Before you listen, make sure you understand these words.

convenience store	battery-powered saw	collapse

B. Listen to "Not a Perfect Crime" twice. Write down as many past tense verbs as you can.

_____

_____

_____

_____

C. Work with a partner. Put the sentences in order so they tell the story. Circle the pronunciation of the past tense endings. Then practice telling the story with your partner.

____	He dropped onto the roof.	[əd] / [t] / [d]
____	The roof collapsed.	[əd] / [t] / [d]
____	He climbed the tree.	[əd] / [t] / [d]
____	He drove to the convenience store.	_Irregular verb_
____	He crashed onto the coffee table.	[əd] / [t] / [d]
____	He entered the parking lot behind the store.	[əd] / [t] / [d]
____	The police arrested him.	[əd] / [t] / [d]
____	He turned his car lights off.	[əd] / [t] / [d]
_1_	He decided to rob the convenience store.	([əd]) / [t] / [d]
____	He started to saw a hole in the roof.	[əd] / [t] / [d]

SELF-STUDY

🎧 **First listen to:**
- the words in Exercises 1 and 2.
- the phrases in Exercise 5A.

📼 **Now record them.**

Then record the sentences in Exercise 7C. Say them in the correct order to tell the story "Not a Perfect Crime."

"TH" sounds: [θ] thanks and [ð] that

INTRODUCTION

Look at the pictures. They show you how to say the sounds [θ] and [ð].

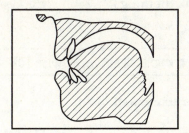 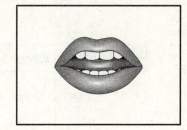

[θ] thanks, three
[ð] that, those

The tip of your tongue is between your teeth.

[θ] is voiceless.
[ð] is voiced.

Spelling for [θ] and [ð]:
th: thanks, thing, author, that, those, mother

- Pronounce the *th* in *cloth,* but do not pronounce the *th* in *clothes.*
  Clothes is pronounced like the verb *close.*

- Pronounce the *th* of *Thai, Thailand,* and *Thames* as [t].

- Final [θ] or [ð] may be simplified or deleted when an *-s* ending is added:

    one mon**th** [θ]—two mon**ths** [ts]
    one-fif**th** [θ]—two-fif**ths** [fs]

FOCUSED PRACTICE

1 LISTEN AND PRACTICE: *TH words with* [θ]

🎧 Listen to these words and repeat them.

1. thing	6. thousand	11. tooth
2. think	7. something	12. mouth
3. thanks	8. healthy	13. fifth
4. theater	9. author	14. bath
5. three	10. nothing	15. death

2 LISTEN AND PRACTICE: *TH words with* [ð]

🎧 Listen to these words and repeat them.

1. this	6. then	11. rather
2. that	7. together	12. bother
3. those	8. other	13. smooth
4. their	9. mother	14. bathe
5. these	10. weather	15. breathe

3 LISTEN FOR DIFFERENCES

🎧 A. Listen to these words and repeat them.

1. a. math	3. a. thin	5. a. then	7. a. three
b. mass	b. tin	b. Zen	b. tree
2. a. with	4. a. breathe	6. a. thanks	8. a. thing
b. wit	b. breeze	b. tanks	b. sing

🎧 B. Listen again and circle the words you hear.

4 GAME: *TH sounds*

👥 Play this game in two teams—Team 1 and Team 2. Give points for correct answers, correctly pronounced.

Team 1: Ask the questions on page 191 to the players on Team 2.

Team 2: Answer the questions with a word or phrase containing the "TH" sound. Then ask Team 1 the questions on page 194.

EXAMPLE

Team 1: What's 30 + 3?

Team 2: *Thirty-three.*

5 SAYING SENTENCES: *TH sounds*

A. Listen to these sentences and repeat them. When you say a sentence, group words into phrases and speak smoothly. The underlined words in the first sentence show one way to group the words.

1. The fourth Thursday of November is Thanksgiving.

2. A "thingamajig" is something whose real name you can't think of.

3. Three hundred thirty-three thousand therapists thought about the new theory of thinking.

4. The thieves threatened three dozen Southern mothers.

5. The theme seems thoughtless to them.

B. Work in small groups. Take turns reading a sentence to the group.

6 INTERVIEWS: *When's your birthday?*

A. Ask your classmates when their birthdays are. Write each student's name and birth date in the chart.

January	February	March	April	May	June
July	August	September	October	November	December

B. Listen to these special birthdays and repeat them.

1. the thirteenth birthday
2. the sixteenth birthday
3. the eighteenth birthday
4. the twentieth birthday
5. the twenty-first birthday

6. the thirtieth birthday
7. the fortieth birthday
8. the fiftieth birthday
9. the seventieth birthday

 C. Work in small groups. Discuss these questions about the birthdays in Part B.

- Why do you think these birthdays are special?
- What birthdays are special in your country?

SELF-STUDY

🎧 **First listen to:**

- the words in Exercises 1 and 2.
- the sentences in Exercise 5.

📼 **Now record them.**

Then choose two birthdays that you think are special. Make a one-minute recording describing why the birthdays are special.

[p] pie, [b] buy, [f] fine, [v] vine, and [w] wine

INTRODUCTION

Look at the pictures. They show you how to say the sounds [p], [b], [f], [v], and [w].

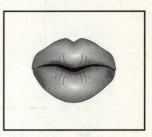

[p] **pie**
[b] **buy**

[f] **fine**
[v] **vine**

[w] **wine**

Close your lips completely to stop the air.

[p] is voiceless
[b] is voiced.

Touch your top teeth gently against the inside of your lower lip.

Your lower lip protrudes a little.

[f] is voiceless.
[v] is voiced.

To make [w] at the beginning of a word, start with your lips rounded. Then unround your lips.

To make [w] at the end of a word, start with your lips unrounded. Then round your lips.

Tips

1. If your native language is Korean, you may pronounce *question* like "kestion." If this is a problem, concentrate on rounding your lips to make the [w] sound.

2. If your native language is Japanese, you may pronounce *woman* and *would* like "'oman" and "'ood." If this is a problem, try these tips:

   • Start with your lips rounded and then unround them as you say *woman*. Unrounding creates [w] at the beginning of a word.
   • Try making two [u] sounds: uuman (woman)
   • Stretch a rubber band as you say the beginning of *woman* and *would*.

Spellings for [p], [b], [f], [v], **and** [w]	

[p], [b], [f], [v], and [w] are usually spelled with the letters *p, b, f, v,* and *w.*
Other
  [f]
    ph: al**ph**abet, tele**ph**one
    gh: enou**gh**, lau**gh**, tou**gh**
  [w]
    u: **q**uestion, s**q**uare, lang**u**age, **q**uiet, pers**u**ade
    wh: **wh**ere, **wh**en, **wh**y, **wh**ile, **wh**ite
    unwritten [w]: once, one
	Silent letters
	Silent *p:*
	  p̸sychology, p̸sychiatrist, receip̸t, cup̸board, rasp̸berry
	Silent *b:*
	  thumb̸, bomb̸, comb̸, climb̸, doub̸t, deb̸t
	Silent *w:*
	  answ̸er, w̸rite, w̸rong, w̸rap, w̸rinkle, w̸reath, w̸hole, w̸ho

FOCUSED PRACTICE

1	**LISTEN AND PRACTICE:** *Words with* [p] *and* [b]

🎧   Listen to these words and repeat them.

	[p]				[b]	
1.	person	5.	cup	9.	best	13. rob
2.	pink	6.	stop	10.	begin	14. somebody
3.	copy	7.	people	11.	lobby	15. Bobby
4.	happy	8.	population	12.	about	16. baby

2	**LISTEN AND PRACTICE:** *Words with* [f] *and* [v]

🎧   Listen to these words and repeat them.

	[f]				[v]	
1.	fix	5.	laugh	9.	very	13. give
2.	finish	6.	belief	10.	voice	14. have
3.	awful	7.	fulfill	11.	never	15. vivid
4.	difficult	8.	falafel*	12.	heaven	16. olive

falafel: a Middle Eastern food made from fried chickpeas and spices

3 LISTEN AND PRACTICE: *Words with* [w]

🎧 Listen to these words and repeat them.

1. woman	4. away	7. quiet
2. would	5. language	8. twenty
3. walk	6. quietly	9. question

4 LISTEN FOR DIFFERENCES: [p] *versus* [b] *versus* [f] *versus* [v] *versus* [w]

🎧 A. Listen to these words and repeat them.

1. a. berry	3. a. bull	5. a. pear
b. very	b. full	b. fair
c. wary*	c. wool	c. wear
2. a. pine	4. a. pest*	6. a. Pow!
b. fine	b. vest	b. vow
c. wine	c. west	c. Wow!

wary: careful; *pest:* a bug or person that bothers you

🎧 B. Listen again and circle the words you hear.

5 LOOK AND LISTEN FOR DIFFERENCES: [p] *versus* [b] *versus* [f] *versus* [v] *versus* [w]

A. Work with a partner. Choose one word from each set in Exercise 4. Face your partner and take turns saying the word without using any sound ("mouth" the word). Use the mouth pictures below to help you. Your partner will decide which word you said by looking at the shape of your mouth.

  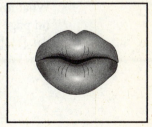

| [p], [b] | [f], [v] | [w] |

B. Repeat the exercise with your partner. This time, say the words aloud.

6 GAME: [p], [b], [f], [v], *and* [w]

Play this game in two teams—Team 1 and Team 2. Give points for correct answers, correctly pronounced.

Team 1: Ask the questions on pages 191–192 to the players on Team 2.
Team 2: Answer the questions with a word that has [p], [b], [f], [v], or [w]. Then ask Team 1 the questions on pages 194–195.

> **EXAMPLE**
>
> **Team 1:** What's the opposite of *answer*?
> **Team 2:** *Question.*

7 LISTENING: *"Phobias"*

A. Before you listen, make sure you understand these words.

> phobia   claustrophobic   panicky   gravity   eggshells   string

B. Listen to "Phobias." Then answer these questions.

1. What is a phobia? _____

2. What is a common phobia? _____

3. What are some rare phobias? _____

8 LISTENING: *Top Ten Phobias*

What are people afraid of? A poll asked Americans about their phobias. The chart on page 75 shows the ten most common phobias. (Bold letters are the sounds [p], [b], [f], [v], or [w].)

Top Ten Phobias*	Rank (1 = most common, 10 = least common)	Do you have this phobia?
Thunderstorms		
Vomiting		
Heights		
Spiders		
Cancer		
People and social situations		
Death		
Flying		
Open spaces		
Confined spaces		

*As reported in *Top 10 of Everything 2001* by Russell Ash

A. Listen to these phobias and repeat them.

B. How do you think Americans ranked the phobias in the chart? What do you think the most common phobia was? Write *1* next to this phobia. Rank the rest of the phobias from 2 to 10. Then check the phobias you have.

C. Work with a partner. Compare your rankings. (You can check your guesses against the Answer Key on page 190.) Why do you think people have these phobias? Do you and your partner have similar phobias?

SELF-STUDY

🎧 **First listen to:**

- the words in Exercises 1, 2, 3, and 4.

📼 **Now record them.**

Then make a one-minute recording about phobias. Use these questions to help you.

- Do you have any of the phobias listed in Exercise 8?

- What other things are you afraid of?

- Are all the phobias in Exercise 8 irrational fears? Why or why not?

UNIT 16 [s] _seven and [z] _zero

INTRODUCTION

Look at the pictures. They show you how to say the sounds [s] and [z].

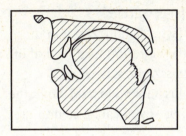 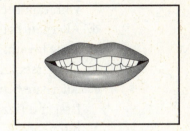

[s] seven
[z] zero

The tip of your tongue is high in your mouth, behind your top teeth.

[s] is voiceless.

[z] is voiced.

Spellings for [s]	Spellings for [z]
Common s: yes, some, this, sister ss: messy, kiss, class, possible se: horse, promise, mouse **Other** c: (before *e, i, y*): cent, city, circle, bicycle, nice, police sc: science, scent, scenery, scissors x (pronounced [ks]): next, excellent, exercise Silent *s:* island, aisle	**Common** z, zz, ze: zoo, crazy, dizzy, size s between vowels: easy, busy, music, visit se: please, rise, because, those **Other** ss: scissors, dessert, possess x (pronounced [gz]): example, exam, exactly, existence

FOCUSED PRACTICE

---

1 SAYING AND FEELING: *Voiced* [z] *and voiceless* [s]

a. Place your fingers against the side of your throat.
b. Make a long [zzzzzz] and feel the vibrations (the voicing).
c. Make a long [ssssss]. You will not feel any vibration because [s] is voiceless.
d. Alternate between [ssssss] and [zzzzzz] in the same breath. Feel the vibration turn on and off.
    [ssssssszzzzzzsssssszzzzzzzsssssszzzzzz]
e. Alternate between [asssa] and [azzza]. Hold the [sss] and [zzz] as long as you can. Listen to the difference.

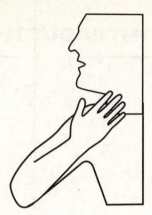

---

2 LISTEN AND PRACTICE: *Words with* [z]

A. Listen to these words and repeat them.

1. busy	5. buzz	9. was	13. easy
2. rose	6. raisin	10. cause	14. wise
3. dizzy	7. noise	11. reason	15. his
4. lazy	8. cousin	12. crazy	16. rising

 B. Work in small groups. Take turns saying four words to the group.

---

3 LISTEN FOR DIFFERENCES: [z] *versus* [s]

A. Listen to these words and repeat them. Then write [z] or [s] to show the sound of the bold letters.

1. choose *[z]*	5. because ___	9. release ___
2. loose ___	6. rose ___	10. please ___
3. music ___	7. dose ___	11. sense ___
4. noise ___	8. chase ___	12. accuse ___

 B. Check your answers with a partner. Practice saying the words.

- Some words end in [s] when they are used as nouns or adjectives and in [z] when they are used as verbs. The vowel before [z] is longer than the vowel before [s].

A. **Listen to these words and repeat them.**

Noun/Adjective: [s]	**Verb:** [z]
1. a use	to use
2. an excuse	to excuse
3. the advice	to advise
4. a choice	to choose
5. a house	to house
6. a close relative	to close the door
7. a loose shirt	to lose something

B. **Fill in the blanks with the words in parentheses.**

1. This three-story _____ can _____ three families.

   (house [s], house [z])

2. _____ carefully so you make the right _____.

   (choice [s], choose [z])

3. Give good _____ when you _____ your friends.

   (advice [s], advise [z])

4. _____ me. I have a good _____ for being late.

   (excuse [s], excuse [z])

5. Don't _____ this phone. It's for office _____ only.

   (use [s], use [z])

C. **Practice reading the sentences with a partner. Pronounce the bold letters [s] when the word is a noun or adjective. Pronounce the bold letters [z] when the word is a verb.**

5 LISTEN FOR DIFFERENCES: [s] *versus* [z]

A. Listen to these words and repeat them.

1. **a.** race		4. **a.** advice		7. **a.** racer		10. **a.** buses
b. raise		**b.** advise		**b.** razor		**b.** buzzes
2. **a.** lease		5. **a.** hiss		8. **a.** loose		11. **a.** noose
b. Lee's		**b.** his		**b.** lose		**b.** news
3. **a.** rice		6. **a.** place		9. **a.** lacy		12. **a.** Miss
b. rise		**b.** plays		**b.** lazy		**b.** Ms.

B. Listen again and circle the words you hear.

6 FILL IN THE GRID

Work with a partner. Each of you has a grid that is partially filled in with words. Student A has the words that are missing from Student B's grid, and Student B has the words that are missing from Student A's grid. Don't show your grid to your partner. Take turns asking each other for missing words. After you are done, compare your grids. They should be the same. Students A's grid is on page 192. Student B's grid is on page 195.

What's in Box A2?

7 LISTEN FOR DIFFERENCES

A. Listen to these sentences and repeat them.

1. **a.** He races cows.

   b. He raises cows.

2. **a.** Here's the racer.

   b. Here's the razor.

3. a. The bus is too loud.

   b. The buzz is too loud.

4. a. I like Miss Evans.

   b. I like Ms. Evans.

5. a. He likes the place.

   b. He likes the plays.

6. a. It's a great price.

   b. It's a great prize.

B. Listen again and circle the sentences you hear.

C. Work with a partner. Use the sentences from Part A to make short dialogues. Use the models below. Pronounce [s] and [z] carefully. When you say B's part, your voice should rise at the end of the question. First listen to the models.

EXAMPLES

A: *He races cows.*

B: Did you say, *"He raises cows?"*

A: No. I said, *"He races cows."*

OR

A: *He races cows.*

B: Did you say, *"He races cows?"*

A: Yes, I did.

SELF-STUDY

First listen to:
- the words in Exercises 2 and 3.
- the sentences in Exercise 7A.

Now record them.

UNIT 17 [ʃ] shoe and [ʒ] televi<u>si</u>on

INTRODUCTION

Look at the pictures. They show you how to say the sounds [ʃ] and [ʒ].

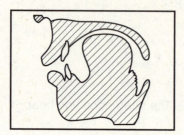 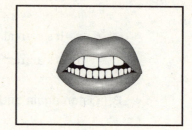

[ʃ] shoe
[ʒ] television

Pull the tip of your tongue back from the front of your mouth.
Your lips protrude a little.

[ʃ] is voiceless.
[ʒ] is voiced.

Spellings for [ʃ]	Spellings for [ʒ]

Common
  sh: **shop, wish, fashion**
Other
  ti: **nation, condition, patient**
  ci: **special, musician, social**
  ssi: **permission, discussion,
    depression**
Unusual
  ma**ch**ine, **Chicago, chic, ocean,
  sure, sugar, insurance, pressure**
	Common
	  si: **decision, vision, television**
	Other
	  su: **casual, treasure, pleasure,
	    measure**
	  ge: **beige, garage, massage**
	Unusual
	  azure

FOCUSED PRACTICE

🎧 Listen to these words and repeat them.

1. shoot	6. glacier	11. cash
2. shine	7. national	12. shy
3. shoe	8. relation	13. wish
4. Chicago	9. vacation	14. push
5. sugar	10. pressure	15. finish

2 LISTEN AND PRACTICE: *Words with* [ʒ]

🎧 Listen to these words and repeat them.

1. decision	5. usual	9. azure
2. pleasure	6. conclusion	10. television
3. Asia	7. measure	11. vision
4. division	8. beige	12. massage

3 SOUNDS AND SPELLINGS

🎧 A. Listen to these words and repeat them.

1. super	5. visit	9. expansion	13. massage
2. sure	6. vision	10. racial	14. ocean
3. casual	7. promising	11. mouse	15. nice
4. result	8. easier	12. museum	16. pleasure

B. Look at the bold letters in the words in Part A. Write each word in the correct column.

[s]	[ʃ]	[z]	[ʒ]
super			

C. Work with a partner. Check your lists. Practice saying the words in each column.

4 DIALOGUES

A. Listen to the sentences in columns A and B. Write the words you hear in the blanks.

A

1. What's the _____ _____, doctor?

2. Where _____ we go on _____?

3. I need to buy some _____ _____.

4. Is there a _____ _____ nearby?

5. You have a lot of tension in your _____.

6. Is there anything _____ on _____?

B

a. I'm under a lot of _____ at work.

b. But, Sheila, don't you hate _____?

c. My _____ is that he has a mild form of _____.

d. No, just the _____ _____.

e. There's one inside the bus _____.

f. I _____ we could visit a _____ park.

B. Work with a partner. Create short dialogues by matching a sentence from column A and a response from column B.

5 VACATIONS

A. Listen to these words and repeat them. The bold letters are [s], [ʃ], [z], or [ʒ].

glaciers	massage	international food	azure water
fashionable people	relaxing	shopping	nutritious food
unusual people	adventure	champagne	Broadway shows
restful	sunshine	expensive	delicious food
inexpensive	museums		

B. Work with a partner. Read the six vacations below. What words do you think of when you think about these vacations? Find words in the box that you associate with these vacations and write them in the blanks. You can use words more than once and add your own words.

1. salmon-fishing in Alaska _____

2. diving for buried treasure in the Caribbean _____

3. staying home, sleeping late, watching television _____

4. a week in New York City _____

5. two weeks at a health spa _____

6. a week in Paris _____

C. Form small groups. Take turns answering the following questions.

- Have you ever been to any of these places?
- What vacations would you like to take?

SELF-STUDY

🎧 **First listen to:**
- the words in Exercises 1 and 2.

📼 **Now record them.**

Then make a one-minute recording describing a vacation you have taken. Where did you go? What did you do? Did you have a good time? Why or why not?

UNIT 18 [tʃ] chicken and [dʒ] jacket

INTRODUCTION

Look at the pictures. They show you how to say the sounds [tʃ] and [dʒ].

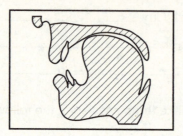 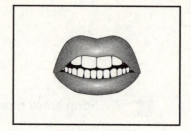

[tʃ] chicken
[dʒ] jet

The tip of your tongue is high and pulled back from your teeth.
Your lips protrude a little.

[tʃ] is voiceless.
[dʒ] is voiced.

Tip

Do you say "wash" when you mean "watch"? If this is a problem, be sure to start the last sound in *watch* with a [t]. You will not hear the [t] as a separate sound.

Spellings for [tʃ]	Spellings for [dʒ]

Common
   ch: **ch**icken, lun**ch**, **ch**ance
   tch: wa**tch**, ma**tch**, ki**tch**en
(In some words, *ch* has a [k] sound: *ache, Christmas, chorus*. In some words, *ch* has a [ʃ] sound: *Chicago, machine*.)
 	
Other
   tu: pic**tu**re, fu**tu**re, na**tu**ral
   ti: ques**ti**on
   c: **c**ello, **c**ellist
	Common
	   j: **j**azz, **J**uly, **j**ust
	   ge: **G**eorge, stran**ge**, colle**ge**
	   dge: bri**dge**, e**dge**, ju**dge**
	
	Other
	   du: gra**du**ate, e**du**cation, indivi**du**al
	   di: sol**di**er

FOCUSED PRACTICE

1   LISTEN AND PRACTICE: *Words with* [tʃ] *and* [dʒ]

🎧   Listen to these words and repeat them.

[tʃ]		[dʒ]	
1. check	5. nature	9. jazz	13. pigeon
2. chalk	6. teacher	10. jacket	14. engine
3. cheap	7. catch	11. gym	15. age
4. kitchen	8. such	12. refrigerator	16. college

2   LISTEN FOR DIFFERENCES: [tʃ] *and* [dʒ] *versus similar sounds*

🎧   A.   Listen to these words and repeat them.

1. a. choice   4. a. mush   7. a. choke
   b. Joyce   b. much   b. joke

2. a. edge   5. a. legion   8. a. cash
   b. etch   b. lesion*   b. catch

3. a. occasion   6. a. H   9. a. pledger*
   b. a Cajun*   b. age   b. pleasure

a Cajun: member of an ethnic group in Louisiana with a French background; *lesion:* a cut or injury to the skin; *pledger:* someone who makes a promise

🎧   B.   Listen again and circle the words you hear.

3   FILL IN THE GRID

👥   Work with a partner. Each of you has a grid that is partially filled in with words. Student A has the words that are missing from Student B's grid, and Student B has the words that are missing from Student A's grid. Don't show your grid to your partner. Take turns asking each other for missing words. After you are done, compare your grids. They should be the same. Students A's grid is on page 192. Student B's grid is on page 195.

4 JOINING FINAL CONSONANTS

A. Review the rules for joining final consonants.

> 1. Join final consonants to following vowels clearly.
> 2. When a final consonant is followed by a different consonant, say the final consonant but keep it short ( )). Then immediately say the next word.

🎧 B. Now listen to these phrases and repeat them. Join words together correctly.

Consonant + Vowel

1. watch a movie
2. a large apartment
3. change a dollar
4. How much is it?

Consonant + Consonant

5. orange) drink
6. age) limit
7. watch) bands
8. strange) noises

5 DIALOGUES

🎧 A. Listen to these questions and answers and repeat them. Follow the intonation lines.

Questions

1. Would you like an orange drink?
2. Do you carry watch bands?
3. Are there any large apartments?
4. Can you change a fifty-dollar bill?
5. How much is that couch?
6. Do you want to watch a movie?
7. Is there an age limit?
8. Did you hear a strange noise?

Answers

a. Yes. But the rent is more.
b. A thousand dollars.
c. No, thanks. I'll just have water.
d. Yes. You have to be 21.
e. No, thanks. I have a headache.
f. Yes, leather and metal.
g. It's just the dog outside.
h. Sorry. I don't have that much.

B. Work with a partner. Create short dialogues by matching a question with an answer from Part A. Practice the dialogues.

6 JOBS

A. Listen to the jobs below and repeat them. What do people with these jobs do?

1. soldier _____
2. jazz pianist _____
3. matchmaker _____
4. store manager _____
5. judge _____
6. teacher _____
7. engineer _____
8. butcher _____
9. forest ranger _____
10. travel agent _____

B. Work with a partner. Read the job characteristics below. What characteristics describe the jobs in Part A? Write the characteristics on the lines, using the words below or your own.

Requires specialized skills/talents—Requires general skills
Common job—Uncommon job
Dangerous/exciting—Quiet/boring
Indoor work—Outdoor work
Competitive/risky—Less competitive/more secure
Well paid—Not (very) well paid

C. Form small groups. Discuss the following questions.

- What are the two best jobs on the list? The two worst jobs? Why?

SELF-STUDY

🎧 **First listen to:**

• the words in Exercises 1 and 2.

• the phrases in Exercise 4.

📼 **Now record them.**

Then make a short recording describing the job you have or one that you would like to have. Is it a good job? Why or why not? Speak clearly and smoothly.

UNIT 19 — "S" endings: plurals, present tense, and possessives

INTRODUCTION

The "S" ending has three pronunciations: [əz]/[ɪz], [s], or [z]. The pronunciation depends on the last sound of the verb or noun.

Pronunciations of the "S" ending

If the last sound is . . .	pronounce the "S" ending . . .	Examples
an "S-like" sound: [s], [z], [ʃ], [ʒ], [tʃ], or [dʒ]	as a new syllable: [əz]/[ɪz]	one boss—two bosses one watch—two watches
a voiceless consonant [p, t, k, θ, f]	as a final sound: [s]	one book—two books I walk—he walks
a voiced consonant or a vowel [b, d, g, ð, v, n, m, ŋ, r, l]	as a final sound: [z]	one dog—two dogs Joe—Joe's

Other Rules

- Many nouns that end in [f] change [f] to [v] in the plural. The plural is pronounced [z].

    knife   knives   half   halves   leaf   leaves

- Some nouns that end in [f] form verbs that end in [v]. Pronounce the present ending [z] if the verb ends in [v]. Pronounce the present ending [s] if the verb ends in [f].

    he believes (noun: belief)   he proves (noun: proof)
    he laughs   she coughs

- When a noun ends in [θ], pronounce the plural ending [s]. Many speakers drop [θ] when it is followed by plural -s. They may lengthen the plural [s] to hold the place of [θ].

    month   months [mənts]   fifth   fifths [fɪfθs] or [fɪfss]

Clothes is pronounced like the verb *to close*.

- When a verb ends in [ð], pronounce the present ending [z]. Many speakers drop [ð] before the ending and make the ending a long [z].

bathe   bathes [beyðz] or [beyzz]   breathe   breathes [briyðz] or [briyzz]

FOCUSED PRACTICE

I	**LISTEN FOR SYLLABLES:** *"S" endings*

🎧 Listen to these words and repeat them. Underline the syllables. Pronounce the ending as a new syllable.

1. **a.** <u>box</u>
   b. <u>box</u><u>es</u>

2. **a.** catch
   b. catches

3. **a.** wish
   b. wishes

4. **a.** dress
   b. dresses

5. **a.** rose
   b. roses

6. **a.** choice
   b. choices

7. **a.** pass
   b. passes

8. **a.** kiss
   b. kisses

9. **a.** age
   b. ages

2	**HOW DOES IT SOUND?**

🎧 **A.** Listen to these nouns. Write the plural noun in the first column. Write the pronunciation of the ending in the second column.

	Plural	**[əz]/[ɪz], [s], or [z]**
1. book	*books*	*[s]*
2. tax		
3. smile		
4. sandwich		
5. window		
6. prize		
7. leaf		
8. hat		

	Plural	[əz]/[ɪz], [s], or [z]
9. exercise	_____	_____
10. mother	_____	_____
11. state	_____	_____
12. month	_____	_____

B. **Check your answers with a partner. Then practice saying the plural nouns.**

3 LISTENING: *Identical twins*

A. **Bruno and Marko Kistler are identical twins. First read the phrases. Then listen to the recording. Do the phrases describe Bruno, Marko, both brothers, or neither of the brothers? Check the information you hear about the brothers.**

	Bruno	Marko
1. have dark, curly hair	____	____
2. have short hair	____	____
3. shave	____	____
4. wear contact lenses	____	____
5. wear glasses	____	____
6. design Web pages	____	____
7. ski	____	____
8. like to dance	____	____
9. play the piano	____	____
10. play the guitar	____	____
11. eat only vegetables	____	____
12. have a girlfriend	____	____

B. **Check your answers with a partner. Then take turns describing the brothers. Use the information in the chart. Use complete sentences and pronounce "S" endings correctly.**

EXAMPLE

Bruno and Marko both have dark, curly hair.

4 U.S. GOVERNMENT AND VERB ENDINGS

The U.S. government has three branches. The executive branch includes the president, his cabinet, and agencies like the FBI. The legislative branch is also known as Congress: it consists of the House of Representatives and the Senate. The judicial branch includes the courts. The three branches have separate functions and powers. The list below gives information about the three branches of government.

 A. Work with a partner. Take turns saying a singular or plural subject. Your partner will make a sentence using the subject. Pronounce the subject carefully so that your partner knows whether to use the verb ending *-s*.

> **EXAMPLE**
>
> **A:** *The president.*
>
> **B:** *The president lives in the White House.*

Subjects	Verb phrases
1. the president/presidents	live in the White House
2. a representative/representatives	serve for two years
3. a senator/senators	serve for six years
4. a Supreme Court justice/Supreme Court justices	serve for life
5. Congress/the House and the Senate	make laws
6. the president/presidents	appoint judges to the Supreme Court
7. the Senate/senators	approve appointments to the Court
8. the president/presidents	make treaties with other countries
9. Congress/the House and Senate	approve treaties made by the president
10. the vice president/vice presidents	serve as the head of the Senate
11. the vice president/vice presidents	vote only when the Senate is tied
12. the House/representatives	initiate legislation to spend money

	Subjects	Verb phrases
13.	the Senate/senators	vote on this legislation
14.	the president/presidents	have the power to veto legislation passed by Congress
15.	the president/presidents	serve as commander-in-chief of the armed forces
16.	the president/presidents	appoint members of the cabinet

 B. Write three sentences about the organization of the government in your country. Then work in small groups. Report the information to your group. Is the organization of your government similar to that of the government of the United States? Explain.

_____

_____

_____

SELF-STUDY

 First listen to:

- the words in Exercises 1 and 2.

Now record them.

Then choose a friend or relative you know well. Record a description of that person. What does the person look like? What does the person do? What are the person's likes and dislikes? Use present tense verbs and pronounce endings carefully.

UNIT 20 [r] _right and [l] _light

INTRODUCTION

Look at the pictures. They show you how to say the sounds [r] and [l].

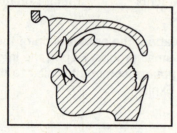

[r] right, **road**

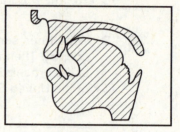

[l] light, **left**

Start with the tip of your tongue turned up and back. Then lower the tip of your tongue.

When you lower the tip of your tongue, do not touch the top of your mouth.

Touch the tip of your tongue just behind the top teeth.

Tips

- [r] is a "movement" sound: The tongue moves out of a turned-back position. It does not touch the top of the mouth.
- [l] is a "contact" sound: The tip of the tongue touches behind the top teeth.

Spellings for [r] and [l]
[r] and [l] are usually spelled with the letters *r* and *l*.
Silent *l*: walk, talk, chalk, half, calf, would, could, should, yolk, calm, palm

FOCUSED PRACTICE

▋1 LISTEN AND PRACTICE: *Words with* [r]

🎧 Listen to these words and repeat them. Start with the tip of your tongue turned up and back. Lower the tip of your tongue. Do not let the tip of your tongue touch the top of your mouth as it lowers.

1. right	5. rich	9. sorry
2. red	6. ready	10. crime
3. room	7. arrive	11. try
4. repeat	8. correct	12. crowd

▋2 LISTEN AND PRACTICE: *Words with* [l]

🎧 Listen to these words and repeat them. Touch the tip of your tongue behind your top teeth.

1. light	5. like	9. collect
2. long	6. listen	10. climb
3. last	7. a lot	11. fly
4. love	8. alive	12. cloud

▋3 LISTEN FOR DIFFERENCES: [r] *versus* [l]

🎧 A. Listen to these words and repeat them.

1. a. lay	3. a. alive	5. a. glass	7. a. Ellie
b. Ray	b. arrive	b. grass	b. airy
2. a. Willy	4. a. list	6. a. climb	8. a. light
b. weary	b. wrist	b. crime	b. right

🎧 B. Listen again and circle the words you hear.

C. Work with a partner. Take turns saying one of the words in Part A. Your partner will tell you which word you said.

LISTEN AND PRACTICE: *Words with* [r] *and* [l]

 A. Listen to these words and repeat them.

1. really
2. slippery
3. salary
4. library

5. electricity
6. laboratory
7. relatives
8. liberate

9. parallel
10. realistic
11. military
12. celebrate

B. Work in small groups. Take turns saying four words to the group.

5 **DIFFERENCES IN MEANING**

A. First look at the road map of Logan. Then listen to these sentences and repeat them.

1. Logan Road is the main road in the town of Logan.
2. Logan Road runs north and south.
3. Rocket Road and Locket Road run east and west.
4. Glassy Lane and Grassy Lane run north and south.
5. Myla's Drive and Myra's Drive also run north and south.
6. There are twelve businesses on Glassy Lane, Grassy Lane, Myla's Drive, and Myra's Drive.

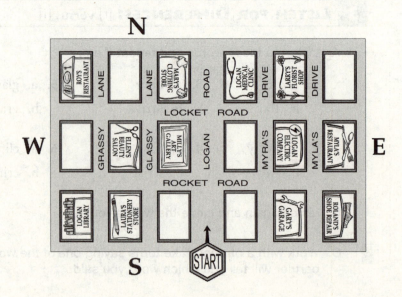

B. Work with a partner. Choose a place in Logan. Don't tell your partner the name of the place. Give your partner directions to get to the place, using the model below. Pronounce [r] and [l] carefully so your partner knows which street to turn on. First listen to the example.

EXAMPLE

   A: Go north on Logan Road. Turn *right* on *Locket Road.*

                                        (right/left)   (road name)

          Then turn *left* on *Myla's Drive.* Where are you?

          (right/left)   (road name)

   B: I'm at *Larry's Florist Shop.*

                 (business name)

6 COUNTRIES

 A. Work in groups of four or five. List as many countries as you can that have [r] or [l] in their names.

Europe	Middle East	Asia	Latin America	Africa
France	Lebanon	Korea	Colombia	Morocco

 B. Now choose a country that you would like to visit and tell your group why. Pronounce [r] and [l] carefully. You can use some of the phrases from the box.

I'd like to go to/travel to	interesting place(s)	friendly people
historical place(s)	really beautiful scenery	culturally rich
island(s), rivers, lakes	a lot of things to do	delicious food

🎧 **First listen to:**

- the words in Exercises 1, 2, and 4.

📼 **Now record them.**

Then record directions to the places below using the map in Exercise 5.

EXAMPLE

Here are directions to *Roy's Restaurant*. First, drive *north* on *Logan Road*. Turn *left* on *Locket Road*. Then turn *right* on *Grassy Lane*. You'll see *Roy's Restaurant* on your *left*.

a. Myla's Restaurant

b. Laura's Stationery Store

c. Gary's Garage

d. Logan Medical Clinic

INTRODUCTION

- [m], [n], and [ŋ] are nasal (nose) sounds. The air comes through the nose.

Look at the pictures. They show you how to say the sounds [m], [n], and [ŋ].

[m] **m**ouse, ho**m**e

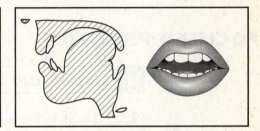

[n] **n**ose, **n**i**n**e

[ŋ] si**ng**, lo**ng**

Close your lips.
The air passes out
through your
nose.

Touch the tip of your tongue
behind the top teeth.
The air passes out through your
nose.

Raise the back of your tongue.
The tip of your tongue is in the
bottom of your mouth.
The air passes out through your nose.
[ŋ] never begins a word.

Tips

1. In many words with -*ng* spellings, *g* is not pronounced. For example, *sing* does not have a [g] sound. In some words, like *finger*, *g* is pronounced as [g].
2. Adjectives that end in [ŋ] add [g] in the comparative and superlative: *long* [ŋ], *longer* [ŋg], *longest* [ŋg].
3. Pronounce nasal consonants clearly when they end words. In some languages, nasal consonants after vowels "nasalize" the vowel, and the nasal consonant can be dropped. In English, however, nasal consonants must be clearly pronounced.
4. Join final nasal consonants to following vowels.

hum‿a song   run‿away   sing‿alto

Spellings for [m]	Spellings for [n]	Spellings for [ŋ]

Common
    m, mm: **m**ouse, **M**o**m**,
    su**mm**er, s**m**all
Other
    mn (silent *n*): autu**mn**,
    hy**mn**
	Common
	    n, nn: **n**ose, s**n**ake, su**nn**y,
	    no**n**e
	Other
	    kn, gn: **kn**ow, **kn**ee, **kn**ife,
	    forei**gn**, si**gn**
		Common
		    ng: si**ng**, ri**ng**ing, wro**ng**,
		    you**ng**
		n before g, k: E**n**glish, a**n**gry,
		    ba**n**k, thi**n**k

FOCUSED PRACTICE

1 | LISTEN AND PRACTICE: *Words with nasal consonants*

Listen to these words and repeat them.

[m]	[n]	[ŋ]	[ŋg], [ŋk]
1. most	7. nail	13. sing	19. drink
2. messy	8. necessary	14. wrong	20. thank
3. imported	9. friendly	15. ring	21. bank
4. stomach	10. happen	16. hanging	22. anger
5. some	11. poison	17. Ping-Pong	23. longer
6. home	12. done	18. young	24. younger

2 | LISTEN FOR SOUNDS: [g] *and* [k]

Listen to these words and repeat them. Write *yes* in the blank if you hear a [g] sound. Write *no* if you do not.

1. fang* _no_   4. strongest ____   7. linger* ____

2. longer ____   5. a strong army ____   8. gang* ____

3. ringing ____   6. hang it up ____   9. clanging* ____

*fang: long, sharp tooth of an animal; *linger:* stay longer; *gang:* group of people;
clanging: loud sound of metal being hit

3 BINGO: *Words with* [m], [n], *and* [ŋ]

A. Listen to the words on the Bingo card and repeat them. Write [m], [n], or [ŋ] under each word.

1. ring *[ŋ]*	**6.** Tim	**11.** Jan	**16.** sinner
2. hang	**7.** sung	**12.** king	**17.** simmer*
3. kin*	**8.** jam	**13.** singer	**18.** sun
4. bang	**9.** Kim	**14.** some	**19.** Bam!
5. rim*	**10.** ban	**15.** tin	**20.** ham

*kin: a relative; *rim*: edge; *simmer*: boil gently

B. Now play Bingo. Use the card in Part A. Listen carefully and cross out each word you hear. When you have crossed out a complete row or column [grid icon] [grid icon], say "Bingo!"

4 DIALOGUES

A. Listen to this dialogue and repeat the lines. Pronounce nasal consonants clearly. Group words together and speak smoothly.

Lucy: I don't have to work tomorrow, so let's do something fun.

Max: What do you want to do? See a movie? Go shopping?

Lucy: Window-shopping, maybe—I'm broke! No, let's do something more fun. Something different. Something outdoors.

Max: We could go to the beach. It's supposed to be warm tomorrow. We could take a picnic lunch and go swimming.

Lucy: That sounds good. We can take the bus there, can't we? I don't want to drive the car on the highway.

Max: The bus? That'll take forever. The car will be fine. The tires aren't that bad. You're worrying again.

Lucy: Someone has to!

B. Work with a partner. Practice the dialogue in Part A.

5 LISTENING: *Top ten tourist activities*

What do tourists like to do? A poll asked Americans what their favorite tourist activities were. The chart below shows the top ten responses.

A. Listen to these tourist activities and repeat them.

Top ten tourist activities	Poll rank (1 = most popular, 10 = least popular)	Which do you enjoy?
Nightlife, dancing		
Going to the beach		
Shopping		
Attending cultural events		
Attending sports events		
Outdoor activities (hiking, fishing, etc.)		
Going to museums and historical sites		
Gambling		
Visiting national parks		
Going to theme parks		

B. How do you think Americans ranked the tourist activities in the chart? What do you think the most common or popular activity was? Write *1* next to this activity. Rank the rest of the activities from *2* to *10*. Then check four activities you enjoy doing when you travel or have free time. Write two other activities that you enjoy doing at the bottom of the chart.

C. Work with a partner. Compare your rankings. (You can check your guesses about the poll rank in the Answer Key on page 190.) Do you and your partner enjoy similar activities?

SELF-STUDY

🎧 **First listen to:**

• the words in Exercises 1 and 2.

📼 **Now record them.**

Then look at the activities below. Which ones do you like doing?

Which ones don't you like? Make a recording of your sentences.

Pronounce nasals carefully.

doing the dishes	cleaning	studying
dancing	eating	cooking
listening to music	talking on the phone	shopping
playing sports	working out	watching TV
reading	gardening	reading

EXAMPLE

I like eating, but I don't like cooking.

[y] <u>y</u>et and [dʒ] <u>j</u>et
Consonant clusters
with [y] re<u>gu</u>lar

INTRODUCTION

Look at the pictures. They show you how to say the sounds [y] and [dʒ].

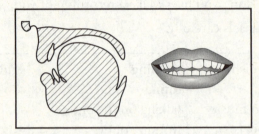

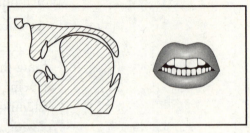

[y] <u>y</u>et, <u>y</u>ou
The center of your tongue slides up
toward the front of your mouth.

[dʒ] <u>j</u>et, <u>g</u>eneral
Keep the tip of your tongue high and
pull it back in your mouth.
The lips protrude slightly.
[dʒ] starts with a [d] sound.

Tips

1. [y] is the second sound in several consonant clusters (consonant groups).
   The [y] sound is usually not written in consonant clusters. When a vowel
   following these clusters is unstressed, it is pronounced [ə].

   re**gu**lar [gyə]   parti**cu**lar [kyə]   voca**bu**lary [byə]   po**pu**lar [pyə]

2. [y] is the last sound of several vowels.

   my [ay]   enj**oy** [oy]   s**ee** [iy]   s**ay** [ey]

   When these vowels are followed by another vowel, join [y] to the next
   vowel.

   my‿uncle   enjoy‿it   see‿ᵞit   say‿it

3. If your native language is Spanish, you may pronounce *yet* like "jet." If
   this is a problem, start [y] words with a long vowel: iiiiiiies (*yes*).

4. Some students pronounce *year* like "ear" and *yield* like "eeled." If this is a
   problem, slide your tongue forward when you say these words.

Spellings for [y]			
Common			

    y: **y**ellow, **y**ard, **y**awn, be**y**ond

    u (at the beginning of some words, but not in the prefix *un-*): **u**se, **u**nion

    u (after *n* and *l* if *u* is unstressed): Ja**nu**ary, va**lu**e, vo**lu**me

    u (after [p, b, m, f, k, g, h] when the preceding vowel is stressed): po**pu**lar,
        am**bu**lance, **mu**sic, **fu**ture, ex**cu**se, ar**gu**e, **hu**mor

    i (after *n* and *l* if *i* is unstressed): o**ni**on, conve**ni**ent, fami**li**ar, mi**lli**on

    ew, iew (pronounced [yuw]): **few**, v**iew**

    eau (pronounced [yuw]): **beau**tiful

Spellings for [dʒ]

See Unit 18.

FOCUSED PRACTICE

1   LISTEN AND PRACTICE: *Words with* [y]

🎧   Listen to these words and repeat them.

1. year	5. yard	9. yesterday	13. useful
2. united	6. beyond	10. young	14. yolk
3. yell	7. yet	11. yield	15. yogurt
4. yeast	8. usual	12. university	16. youth

2   LISTEN FOR DIFFERENCES: [y] *versus* [dʒ]

🎧   A. Listen to these words and repeat them.

1. **a.** yes	4. **a.** yawn	7. **a.** yellow
b. Jess	**b.** John	**b.** Jell-O™
2. **a.** yolk	5. **a.** year	8. **a.** use (noun)
b. joke	**b.** jeer*	**b.** juice
3. **a.** yet	6. **a.** Yale	9. **a.** year
b. jet	**b.** jail	**b.** ear

jeer: make fun of someone, showing disrespect; shout disrespectfully

🎧 B. Listen again and circle the words you hear.

3 CONSONANT CLUSTERS

🎧 The bold letters in the words below are consonant clusters with [y]. Listen to these words and repeat them.

1. com**pu**ter	5. m**u**sic	9. voca**bu**lary
2. **Hou**ston	6. par**ti**cular	10. **beau**tiful
3. inter**vie**w	7. pe**cu**liar	11. re**gu**lar
4. opi**ni**on	8. pop**u**lation	12. fi**gu**re

4 SAYING SENTENCES

🎧 Listen to these sentences and repeat them. Group words together and speak smoothly.

1. You can't go to Yale if you're in jail.
2. Yellow Jell-O™ usually has a lemon flavor.
3. Yes, Jess made John yawn.
4. He used young jungle animals in his film this year.
5. If you go to the store, I could use some juice, some yams, some jam, and some yeast.

5 LISTENING: *Computer use*

A. Before listening, make sure you understand the vocabulary below. Then read the sentences and questions below that you will answer in Part B.

decade	century	estimate	sixfold increase
huge	steadily	revolutionize	invest

1. In 1990 there were _____ computers in the world.

2. In 2000 there were _____ computers in the world.

3. In what countries are more than half the world's computers?

_____

4. What are three reasons computer use has increased?

_____

🎧 B. Now listen to the recording and complete the sentences and answer the questions in Part A.

---

6   INTERVIEWS: *How do you use computers?*

Work with a partner. Find out how your partner uses computers. Ask your partner these questions and write the answers.

1. Do you use computers . . . ?

    a. to e-mail others _____   **h.** for investing _____

    b. for shopping _____   **i.** to take courses _____

    c. for booking tickets _____   **j.** for writing _____

    d. to listen to music _____   **k.** for art/design _____

    e. to watch movies _____   **l.** for research/information _____

    f. for banking _____   **m.** other _____

    g. for meeting people _____

2. Do you think computers save time? Why or why not?

    _____

    _____

3. Do you think computers save money?

    _____

SELF-STUDY

🎧 **First listen to:**
- the words in Exercises 1, 2, and 3.

📼 **Now record them.**

Then make a one-minute recording about your computer use.

If you don't use a computer, explain why not. If you use a computer, what do you use it for?

INTRODUCTION

Look at the picture. It shows you how to say the sound [h].

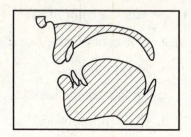

[h] **h**at, a**h**ead

[h] is similar to the sound of
breathing after exercise.

The back of your tongue should not
be close to the top of your mouth.

Tips

1. The letter *h* is never pronounced in these words, which begin with vowel sounds:

   h̸our   h̸onest   h̸onor   h̸eir   h̸erb

   Use the article *an* with these words:

   an h̸our   an h̸onest man

2. The letter *h* is not pronounced in these words:

   veh̸icle   exh̸aust   exh̸ibit

3. [h] is often dropped in *he, him, his, her, have, has,* and *had* when they are unstressed inside a sentence. When *h* is "dropped," the rest of the word joins to the preceding word. If it is difficult for you to pronounce these reductions and join the words together, you can pronounce the words with [h].

   What did h̸e give h̸er? (say "What diddy giver?")

4. [h] is never dropped when *he, him, his, her, have, has,* and *had* begin a sentence. [h] is never dropped in short answers with *have, has,* or *had*.

   He left.   Her name is Joan.   Have you seen it? Yes, I have.

Spellings for [h]
Common
h: **h**ungry, **h**eart, **h**old, in**h**erit
Other
wh: **wh**o, **wh**ose, **wh**om, **wh**ole
Silent *h:*
~~h~~our, ~~h~~onest, ~~h~~onor, ~~h~~eir, ~~h~~erb, ve~~h~~icle, ex~~h~~aust, ex~~h~~ibit

FOCUSED PRACTICE

1   LISTEN AND PRACTICE: *Words with* [h]

Listen to these words and repeat them.

1. happen	4. behind	7. overhear	10. inhale
2. healthy	5. home	8. harmful	11. ahead
3. house	6. inhabit	9. hint	12. humor

2   SOUNDS AND SPELLING

Listen to these words and repeat them. Draw a line through the letter *h* if it is not pronounced.

1. hour	5. heavy	9. unhappy	13. vehicle
2. head	6. behind	10. alcohol	14. hot
3. humid	7. honesty	11. honorable	15. however
4. herb	8. inherit	12. behave	16. heir

3   DIFFERENCES IN MEANING

Work with a partner and take turns. Read either sentence *a* or sentence *b* to your partner. Pronounce the words carefully so your partner can read the correct response to you.

Sentences	Responses
1. **a.** I ate ice cream.	You'll never lose weight eating that way!
b. I hate ice cream.	Really? Most people love it.

continued

Sentences	**Responses**

2. a. Do you use hair spray? No, it makes my hair sticky.

   b. Do you use air spray? No, I just open a window.

3. a. Did you hear that howl? Yes, there must be coyotes around.

   b. Did you hear that owl?   Yes, it lives in the big tree beside the house.

4. a. The heart organization put out this booklet. It urges people to eat less fat and exercise regularly.

   b. The art organization put out this booklet. It describes the new exhibit at the museum.

5. a. Please eat up the chicken. I can't. I'm allergic to it.

   b. Please heat up the chicken. It's much better served cold.

4 REDUCTIONS OF "H" WORDS

Listen to these sentences and repeat them. Pronounce the underlined words as one word. Do not pronounce *h*.

1. What did he do? (say "diddy")

2. What's his name? (say "whatsız")

3. Where has he gone? (say "whərəziy")

4. Watch her. (say "watcher")

5. Look him in the eye. (say "lookım")

6. What have you done? (say "whatəv")

5 SOUNDS LIKE . . .

A. Homophrases are two phrases that sound the same but have different meanings and spellings. Listen to these phrases and repeat them.

1. Did you say "catcher"? _Did you say "catch her"?_

2. Izzy Cumming _____

3. canny* driver _____

4. Woody Walker Katz _____

5. Oliver Boots _____

6. the delays of Koster Munny _____

7. The actresses left. _____

canny: clever

B. Work with a partner. Take turns saying each phrase in Part A. Find another phrase with *he, his, him, her, have, has,* or *had* that sounds the same and write it in the blank. Hints: a *-y* ending could be *he;* an *-er* ending could be *her;* an *-es* ending could be *has;* and *of* could be *have.* (You can check your answers on page 190.)

6 THE WEATHER

A. Listen to these words and repeat them. Make sure you understand the vocabulary.

high heat	tornadoes	high winds	fair
high humidity	hurricanes	breezy	blizzard
cool	drizzle	calm	hail
thunder and lightning	downpours	warm	showers

B. Work with a partner. Do the words in the box describe extreme or severe weather conditions, or do they describe mild weather conditions? Write the words from the box in the columns below.

Extreme weather   **Mild weather**

high heat   _____

_____   _____

_____   _____

_____   _____

_____   _____

_____   _____

_____   _____

Work in large groups and complete the chart. Talk about the weather. Ask questions and write the names of classmates who answer "Yes." Whose name appears most often on the chart?

EXAMPLES
Have you ever been in a *hurricane*?
Do you like *heat and humidity*?

Find someone who . . .	Name
1. has been in a hurricane, cyclone, typhoon, blizzard, etc.	
2. likes heat and humidity	
3. likes high heat but low humidity	
4. likes cold winters with lots of snow	
5. prefers four distinct seasons	
6. prefers year-round mild temperatures	
7. likes to watch weather reports or the weather channel	
8. thinks storms are exciting	

SELF-STUDY

🎧 **First listen to:**

- the words in Exercises 1 and 2.
- the sentences in Exercise 4.

📼 **Now record them.**

Then make a short recording of your answers to these questions.

- How do these weather conditions affect people?

  —days of rain with no sunshine

  —a long period of high heat and humidity

- Does the weather affect your mood? How?

INTRODUCTION

Pronounce the consonants in consonant clusters (groups of consonants) closely together. Do not separate them with a vowel sound.

Listen to the difference between the words in Column 1 and the words in Column 2.

Consonant cluster	Consonant + vowel
prayed	**pa**rade
claps	**co**llapse
sport	**su**pport

- Clusters with [s]

spot	**st**ay	**sc**ore	**sm**all	**sn**ake	**sw**ing
slow	**spr**ing	**spl**it	**str**ong	**scr**eam	**sw**eater

- Clusters with [r] and [l]

pray	**pl**ay	**br**eak	**bl**ue	**tr**ain	**dr**ive	**cr**y
climb	**gr**ow	**gl**ass	**thr**ee	**fr**ee	**fl**y	**sl**eep

- Clusters with [w]

twelve	**dw**ell	**qu**ick	**Gw**en	**sw**ear	**qu**estion

- Rare clusters. These clusters occur in only a few words.

[ʃr]	**shr**ink	**shr**ub	**shr**ivel
[sf]	**sph**ere		

Tips

1. If your native language is Spanish, make sure you do not add a short [ɛ] sound before [s] clusters. If this is a problem, practice [s] clusters by holding a long [sssss] and then pronouncing the rest of the word: *ssstate.*

   state (not "estate")   steam (not "esteem")

2. If your native language is Korean, you may not pronounce the [w] sound in [kw] clusters strongly enough: *question* [kwɛstʃən]. If this is a problem, round your lips as you make the [k] sound, and unround them as you pronounce the vowel.

FOCUSED PRACTICE

I LISTEN AND PRACTICE: *Words with clusters*

🎧 **A.** Listen to these words and repeat them.

1. smell	7. gray	13. flower	19. question
2. stay	8. brown	14. glad	20. quiet
3. snow	9. throw	15. flat	21. quick
4. stranger	10. tree	16. cloudy	22. twin
5. splendid	11. draw	17. plant	23. Gwen
6. school	12. frighten	18. blouse	24. shrink

 B. Work in small groups. Take turns reading two words from each column to the group.

2 LISTEN FOR DIFFERENCES

🎧 **A.** Listen to these words and repeat them.

1. **a.** parade	4. **a.** state	7. **a.** claps	10. **a.** grass
b. prayed	**b.** estate	**b.** collapse	**b.** gas
2. **a.** esteem*	5. **a.** Clyde	8. **a.** sport	11. **a.** please
b. steam	**b.** collide	**b.** support	**b.** peas
3. **a.** polite	6. **a.** estrange*	9. **a.** black	12. **a.** kite
b. plight*	**b.** strange	**b.** back	**b.** quite

*esteem: respect or high opinion for someone; *plight:* a difficult situation; *estrange:* keep apart or stay away

🎧 **B.** Listen again and circle the words you hear.

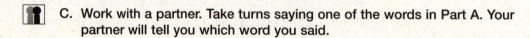 **C.** Work with a partner. Take turns saying one of the words in Part A. Your partner will tell you which word you said.

3 SAYING SENTENCES

A. Listen to these sentences and repeat them. Group words together and speak smoothly.

1. The estate taxes are higher than the state taxes.

2. We prayed the parade would proceed as planned.

3. I scream, you scream, we all scream for ice cream.

4. Answer the quiz questions quickly but quietly, and don't forget to quote the queen.

5. The crowd of clever climbers clad in clean climbing clothes crossed the clearing to the cliff.

B. Work with a partner and practice the sentences.

4 LISTENING: *Personal ads*

Alex Morales and Anita Branca are both unmarried professionals. They spend most of their time working, so they have a hard time meeting people. They both decided to place personal ads in a local newspaper.

A. Before you listen, make sure you understand these words.

athletic	extreme sports	sky-diving	snob
gourmet cooking	slim	ambitious	mature

B. Listen to the ads Alex and Anita placed in the newspaper. Fill in information about Alex and Anita in the chart below.

	Alex	**Anita**
Age		
Marital status, children		
Profession		
Appearance		

continued

	Alex	Anita
Likes		
Dislikes		
Wants to meet someone who . . .		

 C. Work in groups of three. Compare the information in your charts. Discuss the following questions:

- What would Alex and Anita like about each other? What would they dislike? Do you think they would enjoy spending time together?
- Do you know anyone who has placed a personal ad or used a computer dating service to meet another person? What was their experience? Do you think personal ads or computer dating services are good ways to meet new people?

5 PERSONAL ADS

On a separate piece of paper, write a short personal ad for yourself. Do not put your name on your ad. You can use the chart in Exercise 4B as a guide. When you finish, give your ad to your teacher. Your teacher will mix the ads up and give one to each student. Read the ad you get. See if you can figure out who wrote it. Ask your classmates questions about the information in the ad if you aren't sure who wrote it.

SELF-STUDY

First listen to:

- the words in Exercises 1 and 2.
- the sentences in Exercise 3.

Now record them.

Then make a one-minute recording describing how you feel about the idea of meeting people through personal ads or computer dating services. What are some other ways to meet people?

UNIT 25

Final consonant clusters Joining final consonants to the next word

INTRODUCTION

Many English words end in consonant clusters.

> he**lp**   te**st**   la**rge**   gli**mpse**

Verb and noun endings can create new consonant clusters.

> like [k]   li**ked** [kt]
> dog [g]   do**gs** [gz]
> sha**rk** [rk]   sha**rks** [rks]

Words ending in consonants join to the next word in different ways.

- Final Consonant + Vowel. Join a final consonant to a following vowel clearly.

> leave early   hold on   park entrance

- Final Stop Consonant* + Identical Stop Consonant. Hold the final stop consonant briefly. Release it when you say the next word. Do not say the consonant twice.

> great trip   hard day   work quickly

> *stop consonants: [p, b, t, d, k, g]*

- Final Consonant + Identical Consonant. Say one long consonant. Do not say the consonant twice.

> dress simply   enough food   both things

- Final Consonant + Different Consonant. Pronounce the final consonant, but keep it short ('). Say the next word immediately. Do not separate the consonants with a vowel sound.

> sharp' knife   rose' garden   book' bag

continued

- Simplifying Final Clusters. Sometimes a group of three consonants is simplified by dropping the middle consonant. This happens most often when the middle consonant is [p], [t], or [k]. The remaining consonant(s) may be held longer to hold the "place" of the dropped middle consonant. Grammatical endings are never dropped. Look at these examples of final cluster simplifications ([s̄] means [s] is long).

gifts	asked	acts
[gɪfs̄]	[æs̄t]	[æks̄]

- Final Clusters with "TH" Sounds. "TH" sounds are sometimes omitted before plural -s. Final "TH" is not dropped otherwise.

one month	two months	Sixth Street
[nθ]	[nts]	[ks̄]

FOCUSED PRACTICE

1 LISTEN FOR DIFFERENCES: *Final consonant clusters*

A. Listen to these words and repeat them.

1.	**a.** bell		5.	**a.** hole
	b. belt			**b.** hold
2.	**a.** men		6.	**a.** fell
	b. meant			**b.** felt
3.	**a.** car		7.	**a.** were
	b. card			**b.** word
4.	**a.** furs		8.	**a.** lamb
	b. first			**b.** lamp

B. Listen again and circle the words you hear.

C. Work with a partner. Take turns saying one of the words in Part A. Your partner will tell you which word you said.

2 JOINING CONSONANTS

🎧 Listen to these phrases and repeat them.

Consonant + vowel	Consonant + same consonant	Consonant + different consonant
1. correct answer	6. red door	11. junk food
2. expert advice	7. half full	12. walked fast
3. finished early	8. dark clouds	13. health club
4. piles of paper	9. both thumbs	14. change clothes
5. picked it up	10. deep pool	15. bird bath

3 APPLY THE RULE

🎧 The bold letters are consonant clusters that have two or more consonants. Some of the clusters can be simplified. Some cannot be simplified. (You can check your answers on page 190.) Listen to these sentences and repeat them. Did the speaker simplify the consonant clusters? How?

1. He brea**thes** too irregularly.

   "Breathes" is pronounced "breeze," with a long "z."

2. We all brought gi**fts** for my dad's birthday.

   _____

3. The gue**sts** arri**ved** four mo**nths** ago, and they still haven't left!

   _____

4. I a**sked** my boss for a raise. He answe**red** me with a shake of his head.

   _____

5. The responsibility re**sts** with you.

   _____

A. Listen to the sentences in the left column and fill in the blanks.

Sentences

Responses

1. Wait just ten minutes. I have to
   _____ _____ .

   a. Yes. They're old reports from my office. I don't need them anymore.

2. Do you want to _____
   _____ ?

   b. Why don't you come with me to mine tonight? I'm taking a kickboxing class.

3. Did you pick up the tickets at the
   _____ _____ ?

   c. Yes. There's a great movie on channel 5.

4. I'm looking for a _____
   _____ . I want to
   _____ _____ .

   d. Mine wasn't great, either. Let's go shopping. I always feel better when I spend money.

5. Do you have this _____
   _____ in a size ten?

   e. Sorry. Everything we have is on the rack.

6. Have you received my application?
   I sent it a _____
   _____ .

   f. No, you don't. What you're wearing looks great.

7. Let's _____
   _____ . Can I throw
   away these _____
   _____ _____ ?

   g. Hold on a moment. No, we haven't gotten it yet.

8. I had a really _____
   _____ today. How
   was yours?

   h. Yes. The show starts at 8:30, so we'd better leave now.

B. How do the words in the blanks join together? Underline final consonants followed by vowels. Put a long line over and under identical consonants (‿). Put ")" after a final consonant that is followed by a different consonant.

C. Work with a partner. Make short dialogues by matching sentences from the left column with responses from the right. Practice reading the dialogues.

5 DIALOGUE

A. Listen to this dialogue and repeat it. Group words together and speak smoothly.

Sonia: Today was terrible! Everything went wrong today.

Luke: What?

Sonia: I said—everything went wrong!

Luke: What?

Sonia: Well, I lost my keys, I missed my bus, my boss got mad at me, and then—I broke my glasses.

B. Listen again. In Sonia's lines, circle the words with the highest pitch. Draw intonation lines over Luke's questions to show whether his voice is rising (⁄) or falling (＼).

 C. Work with a partner. Practice reading the dialogue.

First listen to:

- the words in Exercise 1.
- the phrases in Exercise 2.

Now record them.

Then record a brief description of a bad day you had. Use your voice to show how you felt and pay attention to the ends of words. Join words together smoothly and clearly. Start your description this way:

"Everything went wrong _____ . . ."

STRESS IN WORDS

INTRODUCTION

Syllables

A syllable is a "beat" of a word. The word *visit* has two syllables, or beats.

v i s i t

Syllable breaks can occur between a vowel and a consonant or between two consonants. It is not important to know exactly where a syllable begins or ends, but it is important to know how many syllables a word has.

vi/sit   fas/ter

Stressed Syllables

One syllable in a word has primary stress (written ´). The vowel in a stressed syllable is longer and louder than vowels in other syllables.

ví sit   fás ter   a gó

I   LISTEN AND PRACTICE: *Hearing stress*

A. Listen to these words and repeat them. Put a stress mark over the stressed syllable (´).

1. desert	dessert	4. decent	descent
2. record (*noun*)	record (*verb*)	5. really	rely
3. message	massage	6. mystic	mistake

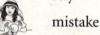

B. Work with a partner. Take turns saying one of the words in Part A. Your partner will tell you which word you said. Pay attention to stressed syllables.

C. Listen to these sentences. Fill in the blanks with the words in parentheses.

1. I had a delicious _____ in the _____. (desert/dessert)

2. They'll _____ the grades in the _____ book. (récord/recórd)

3. Did you say "_____" or "_____"? (rely/really)

4. The spa left a _____ about your _____.
   (massage/message)

5. The _____ made a _____. (mystic/mistake)

D. Work with a partner. Practice reading the sentences in Part C to each other.

Pitch and Stress

Vowels with primary stress are often pronounced on a higher pitch (musical note). In one-syllable words and words stressed on the last syllable, pitch starts high and glides down.

    sad   once   arrive   delay

If unstressed syllables follow the stressed syllable, pitch jumps down.

    visit   happen   travel   kitchen

Unstressed Syllables

Most vowels in unstressed syllables are pronounced [ə] or [ɪ]. Unstressed vowels are short and unclear. They may be spelled with any vowel letter.

contról	agó	diréct	lísten	cáreful
ə	ə	ə	ə	ə

2 LISTEN AND PRACTICE: *Syllable patterns*

A. Listen to these words and repeat them. Tap the syllables with your finger. Underline syllables and write the number of syllables in the blank. Put a stress mark over the stressed syllable (').

1. guitár _2_
2. Alaska ___
3. parents ___
4. enjoy ___

5. tomato ___
6. dinner ___
7. arrangement ___
8. furniture ___

9. musical ___
10. total ___
11. July ___
12. wonderful ___

B. Write each word from Part A under one of the syllable patterns in the chart below (" ′ " means a stressed syllable and " ‿ " means an unstressed syllable.)

Syllable Patterns

′ ‿	‿ ′	′ ‿ ‿	‿ ′ ‿
_____	guitar	_____	_____
_____	_____	_____	_____
_____	_____	_____	_____

3 DIALOGUES

Work with a partner. Make short dialogues by filling in the blanks with words from Exercise 2A. Practice reading the dialogues.

1. **A:** What are we having for _____?
   B: Spaghetti with _____ sauce.

2. **A:** How much was your new _____?
   B: I spent a _____ of $1,000.

3. **A:** Can you play a _____ instrument?
   B: Yes, I play the _____.

4. **A:** When are your _____ coming to visit?
   B: On _____ tenth.

5. **A:** Did you _____ the movie?
   B: Yes! The actors were _____.

Vowel + Vowel Sequences and Syllables

In some words, two vowel letters written together represent one vowel sound.

    br**ea**d   p**ie**ce   b**oa**t   f**ou**r

In other words, two vowel letters represent two vowel sounds that are pronounced in different syllables. The first vowel usually ends in a [w] or [y] sound, for example [iy], [ay], or [uw]. The [w] or [y] is used to join the two vowels together.

    sci^yence   gradu^wate

LISTEN AND PRACTICE: *Hearing syllables*

🎧 Listen to these words and repeat them. Write *1* in the blank if the bold vowel letters are pronounced as one vowel sound. Write *2* if they are pronounced as two vowel sounds, and write the joining sound (*y* or *w*) between the two vowels.

1. br**ea**k __1__   5. soc**ie**ty ____   9. soc**ia**l ____

2. cr**e**ᵞ**a**te __2__   6. bel**ie**ve ____   10. immed**ia**te ____

3. n**eo**n ____   7. qu**ie**t ____   11. z**oo**logy ____

4. p**eo**ple ____   8. s**ui**t ____   12. z**oo** ____

Secondary Stress

Some words have both primary stress and secondary stress (written " ` "). The vowel in a syllable with secondary stress is a full vowel, but it is not pronounced on a high pitch. In noun compounds (noun + noun), the second noun has secondary stress and low pitch. The first noun has primary stress and high pitch.

RÁIL`road        AÍR`port

5 DIFFERENCES IN MEANING

🎧 A. Listen to these compound nouns and adjective-noun phrases, and repeat them.

Compound		Adjective + Noun	
1. White Hòuse		white hóuse	
2. yéllow jàcket		yéllow jácket	
3. bláckbòard		bláck bóard	
4. dárkròom		dárk róom	
5. a rédeye*		a réd éye	

a redeye: an overnight flight

🎧 B. Listen again and circle the words you hear described.

Work with a partner. Each of you has a grid that is partially filled in with words. Student A has the words that are missing from Student B's grid, and Student B has the words that are missing from Student A's grid. Don't show your grid to your partner. Take turns asking each other for missing words. After you are done, compare your grids. They should be the same. Students A's grid is on page 192. Student B's grid is on page 195.

Stressed syllables; Vowel length; Vowel reduction

INTRODUCTION

Syllables

A syllable is a "beat" of a word. The center of a syllable is usually a vowel.

cat	doctor	important
1 beat	2 beats	3 beats

Stress

- Vowels in syllables with primary stress (ʹ) are longer and louder than other vowels. Primary stress is the strongest level of stress in a word. Vowels with primary stress may be pronounced on a high pitch.

  to dáy   stúdent   wónderful

- Unstressed vowels are usually reduced to [ə] or [ɪ]. Unstressed vowels may be spelled with different letters, but they are usually pronounced the same.

Pronunciation:	léssən	chíckən	əccúr	wómən
Spelling:	lesson	chicken	occur	woman

- Some words have syllables with secondary stress (ˋ). Vowels with secondary stress are full vowels (not reduced), but they are not pronounced on a high pitch. You should pay attention to primary stress.

  áirˋport   róomˋmate

FOCUSED PRACTICE

1 LISTEN AND PRACTICE: *Stress patterns*

🎧 Listen to these words and repeat them. Hold the stressed vowels to make them long. (Stretch a rubber band or pretend you are stretching one when you say the stressed vowel.)

1. m u sic
2. p r o mise
3. t r a vel
4. h a ppen
5. oc c u r
6. af r a i d
7. de c i d e
8. to d a y
9. an o ther
10. to m o rrow
11. rem e mber
12. prof e ssor
13. p r e sident
14. n a tional
15. d i fficult
16. b e a u tiful

2 LISTEN FOR DIFFERENCES: *Stress patterns*

🎧 Listen to these words and repeat them. One word in each set has a different stress pattern. Circle the word with the different stress pattern.

1. together, tomorrow, tobacco, terrific, totally
2. pollution, politics, poetry, popular, possible
3. digital, difficult, discussion, distantly, dieting
4. policeman, chocolate, potato, tomato, Alaska
5. dangerous, criminal, accident, importance, practical

3 LISTEN FOR DIFFERENCES: *Syllables*

🎧 A. Listen to these phrases and repeat them. Tap the syllables with your finger.

A	B
1. start working ___	started working ___
2. a practice test ___	a practical test ___
3. go to Dave ___	go today ___
4. rent an apartment ___	rented an apartment ___
5. answer a question ___	answered a question ___
6. center field ___	Senator Field ___
7. mother's folks ___	mother's focus ___
8. not quite ___	not quiet ___

🎧 **B.** Listen again and circle the phrases you hear.

👥 **C.** Work with a partner. Underline the syllables of the phrases in Part A and write the number of syllables in the blank. Practice saying the phrases.

4 UNSTRESSED VOWELS

🎧 **A.** The words below have been "respelled" to show how the unstressed vowels are pronounced. Listen to the words and repeat them.

1. fashən dəsignər
   fashion designer

2. datə anələst
   _____

3. pilət
   _____

4. pəliceman
   _____

5. managər
   _____

6. travəl agənt
   _____

7. prəfessər
   _____

8. cənsultənt
   _____

9. physəcəl therəpəst
   _____

👥 **B.** Write the normal spelling of the words in Part A in the blanks. Check your answers with a partner and practice saying the words to each other. Pronounce the unstressed vowels as [ə]. (Note: Unstressed vowels spelled with the letters *i* or *e* can be pronounced [ə] or [ɪ].)

5 PROFESSIONS

🎧 **A.** Listen to the words in the box and repeat them. Put a stress mark over the stressed syllable (′). Make sure you understand the words.

courageous	intelligent	logical	friendly	creative
honest	curious	articulate	methodical	adaptable
imaginative	patient	competitive	sensitive	observant

👥 **B.** Work in small groups. What characteristics should a police officer have? A lawyer? A fashion designer? Look at the adjectives in the box. Choose four important adjectives for each profession and write them on the lines. Add another profession at the end of the list and write four important characteristics for it.

1. Police officer _____

2. Lawyer _____

3. Fashion designer _____

4. _____ _____

🎧 **First listen to:**
- the words in Exercise 1.
- the phrases in Exercise 3.

▪️▪️ **Now record them.**

Then write sentences for all of the word sets below. Record the sentences. Pronounce stressed and unstressed syllables correctly.

EXAMPLE

dangerous, accident, Washington

There was a dangerous accident in Washington.

1. o'clock, tomorrow, practice, guitar

   _____

2. beautiful, entrance, office

   _____

3. today, lesson, difficult

   _____

4. police, weapon, dangerous, criminal

   _____

Parts of speech; Suffixes; Numbers

INTRODUCTION

Stress and Parts of Speech

- Two-syllable nouns and adjectives: Stress is usually on the first syllable.

  óffice   fáther   húngry   fámous

- Two-syllable verbs: Stress may be on the first or second syllable.

  lísten   prómise   invíte   belíeve

Suffixes

- Primary stress falls on the syllable before these suffixes: *-tion, -sion, -ic, -ical, -ically, -ity, -ian, -ial, -ialize, -ious, -graphy.*

  defíne + tion → definítion   psychólogy + ical → psychológical
  fántasy + ic → fantástic   phóto + graphy → photógraphy

- Primary stress falls on these suffixes: *-ese, -eer/-ier, -ee.*

  Chína + ese → Chinése   móuntain + eer → mountainéer

- Most other suffixes do not change stress in the base word.

  góvern + ment → góvernment   háppy + ness → háppiness
  predíct + able → predíctable   succéss + ful → succéssful

Suffixes with Secondary Stress

- Suffix *-ate.* When *-ate* is a verb ending, it has secondary stress and is pronounced [eyt]. When *-ate* is a noun or an adjective ending, it is unstressed and pronounced [ət].

Verb [eyt]	**Noun/Adjective** [ət]
to dúplicàte	a dúplicate copy
to gráduàte	gráduate school
to éstimàte	an éstimate

continued

- Suffix *-ize:* The suffix *-ize* has secondary stress.

  re´cognìze   re´alìze

___

Numbers

- **Numbers ending in *-teen***

  - Stress *-teen* when a pause follows. The first syllable has secondary stress.

    I need 18 (eìghte´en).

  - Stress the first syllable of a *-teen* number when it is the first part of a year; *-teen* has secondary stress.

    1850 (eìghte´en fi´fty)

  - Many speakers stress the first syllable of a *-teen* number when the next word begins with a stressed syllable; *-teen* has secondary stress.

    18 Main Street (eìghte´en Ma´in Street *or* eìghte´en Ma´in Street)

  - The *t* in *-teen* has a clear [t] sound.

- **Numbers ending in *-ty***

  - The first syllable of *-ty* numbers is always stressed.

    si´xty   ei´ghty

  - The *t* in *-ty* sounds like a "fast d" in American English.

FOCUSED PRACTICE

I LISTEN AND PRACTICE: *Words with suffixes*

Listen to these words and repeat them.

1. ´tion/sion
   a. organization
   b. permission
   c. circulation

2. ´ic
   a. scientific
   b. realistic
   c. fantastic

3. eer/ier´
   a. volunteer
   b. engineer
   c. financier

4. ´ity
   a. publicity
   b. majority
   c. ability

5. ´graphy
   a. biography
   b. photography
   c. geography

6. ´ial
   a. editorial
   b. memorial
   c. official

2 PREDICTING STRESS

A. Listen to the words in column 1 and repeat them. Review the rules for suffixes in the Introduction. Put a stress mark over the stressed vowels in column 2 (´).

column 1	column 2
1. compéte	competítion, compétitive
2. édit	editor, editorial
3. públic	publícity, públicly
4. phótograph	photógraphy, photográphic, photógrapher
5. prófit	profíteer, prófitable, profitabílity
6. círculate	círculatory, circulátion
7. óffice	offícial, ófficer

 B. Check your answers with a partner. Practice saying the words.

3 DIALOGUES

 Work with a partner. Complete the dialogues with the correct form of the word in parentheses. Put a stress mark over the stressed syllable (´). Then practice the dialogues.

1. (circulate)

    a. **A:** If your fingers and feet are always cold, you probably have poor . . . what's it called?

       B: *Circulátion.*

    b. **A:** What does blood do as it travels through the blood vessels?

       B: It _____.

    c. **A:** What's the name of the system of blood vessels and blood in the body?

       B: The _____ system.

continued

2. (photograph)

    a. **A:** What do you call a person who takes pictures?

       B: A _____.

    b. **A:** What's another word for a "picture"?

       B: A _____.

    c. **A:** What classes do you take to learn about taking pictures?

       B: _____ classes.

3. (edit)

    a. **A:** What should you do before turning in an essay?

       B: You should _____ it.

    b. **A:** What do you call newspaper articles that express the writer's opinion?

       B: _____.

    c. **A:** Who makes the decision to print a story in a newspaper?

       B: The _____.

4. (compete)

    a. **A:** When runners race against each other, what are they doing?

       B: They're _____.

    b. **A:** In a pure capitalist system, what must be present?

       B: Free _____ among businesses.

    c. **A:** Why do brothers and sisters sometimes feel jealous of each other?

       B: They're _____.

4 LISTEN FOR DIFFERENCES: -ate endings

🎧 **A. Listen to the words in the box and repeat them. Then fill in the blanks with the word in parentheses. Write [eyt] or [ət] to show how the ending is pronounced.**

Verbs:	duplicate	graduate	estimate	separate
Nouns/adjectives:	duplicate	graduate	estimate	separate

1. (duplicate)

   a. I don't know whether he wants the original or a ***duplicate* [ət]**.

   b. If he wants a _____, I'll have to _____ the original.

2. (graduate)

When you _____ from college, do you want to go to _____ school?

3. (estimate)

I asked the mechanic to _____ the cost of fixing the car, but his _____ was much too high.

4. (separate)

Recycling Rules: Please _____ the bottles from the cans and put them in _____ containers.

👥 **B. Check your answers with a partner. Practice reading the sentences.**

5 LISTEN FOR DIFFERENCES: Numbers with -teen and -ty

🎧 **A. Listen to these pairs and repeat them.**

1. a. 80		**3. a.** 3:40		**5. a.** 5:50	
b. 18		**b.** 3:14		**b.** 5:15	
2. a. 1960		**4. a.** 90		**6. a.** 2050 Main Street	
b. 1916		**b.** 19		**b.** 2015 Main Street	

🎧 **B. Listen again and circle the words you hear.**

6 DIALOGUES

 A. Listen to these dialogues and repeat them. Fill in the blanks with the numbers you hear.

1. **A:** My brother is going to be ___ tomorrow.

   B: ___?! I didn't know you had a brother that old!

   A: Old? ___ is old?

   B: Did you say forty or fourteen?

   A: ___.

2. **A:** The next train to Boston leaves at ___.

   B: I'm sorry—did you say ___ or ___?

   A: ___.

 B. Work with a partner and check your answers. Then practice the dialogues.

7 WHEN DID IT HAPPEN?

Work with a partner. Take turns. Choose a date and ask your partner what happened on that date. Your partner will tell you what happened. Student A's information is on page 192. Student B's information is on page 195.

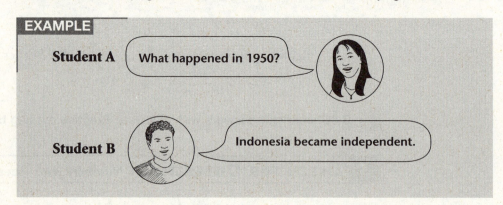

EXAMPLE

Student A — What happened in 1950?

Student B — Indonesia became independent.

First listen to:

- the words in Exercises 1 and 5.

▶️ **Now record them.**

Then write sentences for all of the word sets below. Record the sentences. Pronounce stressed and unstressed syllables correctly.

1. photograph, photographer

_____

2. electric, electricity

_____

3. separate (verb), separate (noun/adjective)

_____

4. public, publicity

_____

INTRODUCTION

Compounds

- Compound nouns are two nouns used together as one noun. Pronounce the first noun with heavy stress and high pitch. Pronounce the second noun with secondary stress and low pitch.

póst office   ráil road   schóol bus

Two-Word Verbs Used as Nouns

- Use the stress-pitch pattern of compound nouns.

The táke off has been delayed an hour.   I bought some new máke up.

Noun-Verb Pairs

- Some two-syllable words are nouns when stress is on the first syllable and verbs when stress is on the second syllable.

Noun	Verb
a récord	to recórd
a cónvict	to convíct
a présent	to presént

Spelling

- Noun compounds may be written as one word or as two words.

railroad	bedroom	roommate	bookstore
library book	night school	bus route	bike path

FOCUSED PRACTICE

1 LISTEN AND PRACTICE: *Compounds*

🎧 Listen to these compounds and repeat them.

1. birth date
2. graduate school
3. White House
4. age limit
5. travel agent
6. employment history
7. fingerprints
8. greenhouse
9. footbridge
10. orange juice
11. driver's license
12. darkroom
13. report card
14. blood type

2 LISTEN FOR DIFFERENCES: *Stress patterns*

🎧 Listen to these phrases and repeat them. Circle the phrase that has the compound stress-pitch pattern (heavy stress and high pitch on the first word; secondary stress and low pitch on the second word).

A	B
1. a blackboard	a black board
2. the post office	the new office
3. paper napkins	paper clips
4. a birthday card	a beautiful card
5. an impressive building	an office building
6. fresh juice	grape juice
7. a lighthouse*	a light color
8. a greenhouse*	a green house

*lighthouse: a tall structure with a powerful light to guide ships; *greenhouse*: an enclosed area for growing plants in cold weather

🎧 **A. Listen to the sentences in the left column and fill in the blanks.**

Sentences   **Responses**

1. Did you use the _____   **a.** Yes. I bought some vitamins.
   to cross the stream?

2. Is that your _____?   **b.** Eighteen years old.

3. Did you go to the _____? **c.** Yes, but I didn't see the
                                          president.

4. What's the _____?   **d.** My flight leaves at 8:00, so
                                          probably 5:30.

5. Did you visit the _____? **e.** Congratulations! I guess you
                                          finally learned to park.

6. I got my _____!   **f.** Yes. That's where I develop my
                                          photographs.

7. What's the _____ for   **g.** Heavy rain and high winds.
   tomorrow?

8. What time do you have to leave   **h.** No, I just took my shoes off
   for the _____?   and walked across.

 **B. Work with a partner. Make short dialogues by matching sentences from the
left column with responses from the right. Practice reading the dialogues.**

🎧 **A. Listen to these words and repeat them.**

Noun	**Verb**	**Noun**	**Verb**
1. **a.** cónvert	**b.** convért	6. **a.** pérmit	**b.** permít
2. **a.** récord	**b.** recórd	7. **a.** présent	**b.** presént
3. **a.** rébel	**b.** rebél	8. **a.** óbject	**b.** objéct
4. **a.** súspect	**b.** suspéct	9. **a.** cóntract	**b.** contráct
5. **a.** cónvict	**b.** convíct	10. **a.** prótest	**b.** protést

🎧 **B. Listen again and circle the words you hear.**

5 NOUN OR VERB?

Fill in the blanks with words from Exercise 4A in their correct forms. Write "'" over the stressed syllable.

1. Doctors keep _____ of their patients' health conditions.

2. At an annual checkup, doctors usually _____ a patient's weight and blood pressure.

3. The United States became an independent country when the original thirteen colonies _____ against British rule.

4. In New York City, empty factory buildings have been _____ into residential lofts.

5. Without a parking _____, you can't park in this lot.

6 RECORDS

Governmental and nongovernmental organizations keep detailed records about many aspects of our lives. The table in Part A shows some types of information that organizations use. Make sure you understand the items in the table.

A. Listen to the phrases in the table and repeat them.

Information	Used for/by:
Blood type	
Credit history	
Medical history	
Employment history	
Birth date	
Fingerprints	
DNA	
School records	
Marital status	
Birthplace	
Dental records	

B. What organizations/people make use of the information in Part A? What is the information used for? Write answers in the table.

 C. Work in small groups. Compare the information in your charts. Discuss answers to these questions.

- What types of information do you think organizations have about you?
- Do you worry that personal information about you may be misused?

SELF-STUDY

🎧 **First listen to:**

- the phrases in Exercises 1 and 2.

📼 **Now record them.**

When you applied to this school, what information did you have to put in the application? If you are an international student, what information did you have to supply to get a visa? Record a brief description of the information you gave. Concentrate on using correct stress patterns.

RHYTHM AND INTONATION

RHYTHM

Rhythm is the patterning of strong and weak (stressed and unstressed) syllables in phrases and sentences.

1 RHYTHM IN POETRY

In poetry, rhythm patterns are repeated and easy to hear. Listen to the first two lines of "The Night before Christmas" by Clement C. Moore. (′ means a strong/stressed syllable and ˘ means a weak/unstressed syllable.)

'Twăs thĕ níght bĕfóre Chrístmăs, whĕn áll thrŏugh thĕ hóuse,

Nŏt ă créatŭre wăs stírrĭng, nŏt évĕn ă móuse.

2 LISTEN AND PRACTICE: *Rhythm in speaking*

A. Regular, repeated rhythm patterns can also occur in speaking. Listen to the dialogue and repeat the lines.

A: Thĕ sófă lóoks ă líttlĕ táttĕred.*

B: Wĕ cán't ăfförd tŏ búy ă néw ŏne.

A: Ĭ knów ă plácĕ thăt sélls ăt díscŏunt.

B: Yŏu méan thĕ plácĕ thăt sóld ŭs thĭs óne?

*tattered: old and torn

 B. Work with a partner. Practice the dialogue.

CONTENT WORDS AND FUNCTION WORDS

Rhythm patterns in sentences are like stress patterns in words. In sentences there are stressed and unstressed words; in words there are stressed and unstressed syllables.

- **Content Words: Stressed Words.** Content words include nouns, verbs, adjectives, and adverbs. Content words have clear meaning and are usually stressed.

  Jóe's láte.

- **Function Words: Unstressed Words.** Function words include articles, prepositions, auxiliary verbs, pronouns, and conjunctions. They are usually unstressed.

  We can DRÍVE to the BÉACH.

---

3 **HEARING RHYTHM**

🎧 A. Listen to the dialogue. Mark stressed syllables (′).

   A: I tóld you to thrów it.

   B: I thought you said kick it.

   A: We're not playing soccer.

   B: Well, I didn't know that!

👥 B. Work with a partner. Practice the dialogue.

TIMING STRESSED SYLLABLES

Speakers "time" their speech so that the amount of time between stressed syllables is about the same.

---

4 **HEARING STRESSED SYLLABLES AND RHYTHM**

🎧 Listen to these sentence sets. The sentences in each set have different numbers of unstressed syllables but the same number of stressed syllables. The sentences in each set should take about the same amount of time to say. The rhythm pattern of the *a* sentences sounds "slower" because there are no unstressed syllables. The rhythm pattern of the *b* and *c* sentences sounds faster because of the unstressed syllables.

			Total Syllables
1. a.	Cláss	stárts	nów.	(3 syllables)
b.	The cláss	is stárting	todáy.	(7 syllables)
c.	The clásses	should be stárting	tomórrow.	(10 syllables)
2. a.	Móm	boúght	shóes.	(3 syllables)
b.	Did Móm	búy	the shóes?	(5 syllables)
c.	Did your Móm	búy you	the shóes?	(7 syllables)

REDUCED WORDS

Native speakers often use reduced pronunciations of certain unstressed words. The vowels in these words are usually reduced to [ə], and consonants may be dropped. The reduced words join closely to surrounding words in the sentence. If you are familiar with these reductions, you will understand spoken English more easily.

5 LISTEN AND PRACTICE: Reduced words

The underlined words in the sentences below have the same pronunciation (or nearly the same). Listen to how the function words are pronounced and repeat the sentences.

1. In the tropics, seas and lakes don't freeze in any season.

2. The first reader can't read or write another language.

3. Did he call Mr. Diddy?

4. If the coffee's too strong, we can weaken it.

5. How much do you need to borrow tomorrow?

6. The baker's going to bake her a special cake.

THOUGHT GROUPS AND JOINING

We break sentences into shorter phrases, or thought groups, to make them more understandable. A thought group has at least one stressed word in it. The words in a thought group are pronounced together smoothly.

at home   walking to school   my friend and I

There are no fixed rules for how long a thought group should be. When you are learning English, you should use shorter thought groups. Look at two ways to group the words in this sentence:

I'm leaving at ten this evening.   I'm leaving at ten this evening.

6 LISTENING

Lucy and Max are newlyweds. A month ago they met in Las Vegas and got married the next day. They are now living in Lucy's studio apartment in Los Angeles.

A. First listen to the messages on their answering machine.

B. Now listen to the phrases in the columns and repeat them. Pronounce the words in each phrase as a thought group.

1	2	3
The phone company	doesn't have any work	about her marriage.
The A1 Modeling Agency	is very upset	for Max.
Lucy's father	wants Lucy to call	as soon as possible.

C. Work with a partner. Match phrases from the three columns in Part B to make sentences that summarize the messages. Practice reading the sentences to each other. Use thought groups and speak smoothly.

HIGHLIGHTING IMPORTANT WORDS

In most sentences, one or two words are the most important to the speaker. The speaker highlights the words by pronouncing them with strong stress, on a high pitch (a high note).

I'm HUN gry.   She's my MO ther.

A. Listen to the dialogue and repeat the lines. Highlight the words in capital letters by pronouncing them with strong stress, on a high pitch.

Max: This apartment is TOO small.

Lucy: It ISN'T. It's FINE.

Max: NO. It's TOO SMALL.

Lucy: It ISN'T.

Max: It IS.

Lucy: It's the BEST we can do for now.

Max: I STILL say it's too SMALL.

Lucy: It doesn't MATTER what you say.

B. Work with a partner. Practice the dialogue.

INTONATION PATTERNS AND SENTENCE TYPES

Intonation is the melody of speech, the pattern of high and low notes.

Certain intonation patterns are often used with particular types of sentences. *Yes/No* questions, for example, often end with rising intonation. Information questions often end with falling intonation. How would you say these questions?

Are you from Brazil?   Where are you from?

INTONATION AND ATTITUDES

Your intonation tells the listener how you feel. If your intonation is flat or monotone, the listener may think that you are bored or unhappy.

8 DIALOGUES

A. Listen to the first line of the dialogues. How do you think B will respond to A's question? Why?

1. **A:** Who bought this chair?

   B: I did—isn't it great?!   OR   Don't you like it?

2. **A:** Who bought this chair?

   B: I did—isn't it great?!   OR   Don't you like it?

B. Work with a partner. Take turns and practice the dialogues. When you say A's part, use intonation so your partner will know how to respond.

9 LISTENING

Sylvia just got a promotion, and she and her husband Jack are going on their first vacation in three years. Jack has made a list of possibilities, and he is reading them to Sylvia. Sylvia doesn't answer Jack with words, but her intonation says how she feels about the suggestions.

A. Listen to Jack and Sylvia. As you listen, check the column that shows how Sylvia feels about the suggestions.

Jack's suggestions	Sylvia's feelings about the suggestions		
	Good	Not sure	Bad
A camping trip?			
A fishing trip?			
Renting a house on the beach?			
A week in New York City?			
A trip to Hawaii?			
Two weeks in Paris?			

B. Write three suggestions for a class trip on the lines below.

1. _____

2. _____

3. _____

C. Work with a partner. Take turns reading your suggestions. Your partner will "hum" a response to each suggestion, using intonation to show how he or she feels. Which suggestions did your partner like?

UNIT 31 Content and function words Thought groups

INTRODUCTION

Rhythm

Rhythm is the alternation of strong (stressed) and weak (unstressed) beats or syllables. Just as words are made up of strong and weak syllables, phrases and sentences are made up of strong and weak words. The rhythm/stress pattern of words and sentences can be the same.

Alaska   I'll ask her.

Content and Function Words

Strong Words or Content Words. Content words are nouns, verbs, adjectives, adverbs, question words, and demonstratives (*this/that/these/those*). These words are usually stressed in a sentence.

I'm RÉADY to ÓRDER.

Weak Words or Function Words. Function words are pronouns, prepositions, auxiliary verbs, conjunctions, and articles. These words are usually unstressed in a sentence. They are short and less clearly pronounced than content words.

We can CÓME at 9:00.

Thought Groups

Sentences are made up of one or more phrases or thought groups. Thought groups help the listener organize the meaning of the sentence. They help the speaker by breaking the sentences into shorter parts. Pronounce words in a thought group together, smoothly.

Some of us are going to leave at 9:00.

Joining Thought Groups. To join thought groups together, hold the end of a thought group briefly before starting the next group. There is also often a small rise in pitch at the end of a thought group.

My flight is arriving at nine o'clock.   I'll call you from the airport.

   ↑   ↑   ↑
 hold   hold   hold

Grammatical Phrases and Thought Groups

Grammatical phrases are often thought groups.

Prepositional phrases:	to the airport	at ten	in the morning
Verb + Pronoun:	bring it	take them	call her
Short clauses:	If you leave, call me.		

FOCUSED PRACTICE

1 LISTEN AND PRACTICE: *Rhythm*

A. Listen to the dialogue and repeat it. Mark stressed syllables (′) and underline thought groups.

Customer: I'm réady to órder.

Waiter: The chicken is yummy.

Customer: I think I'll have waffles.

Waiter: The waffles are awful!

B. Work with a partner. Practice the dialogue. What do you notice about the rhythm pattern of the four lines?

2 DIALOGUES

A. Listen to the first three lines of the dialogues and repeat them.

1. **A:** What's the mátter?

   B: There's no wáter.

   A: Cáll the plúmber.

   B: What's his _____?

2. **A:** I néed your hélp to fíx the cár.

   B: I'll cóme toníght at tén o'clóck.

   A: You sáid befóre you'd cóme at níne.

   B: I'm búsy thén. I'll cóme

   _____.

B. Work with a partner. Complete the last line of the dialogues in Part A. Choose a word (or words) so the last line has the same rhythm pattern as the preceding lines. Practice the dialogues.

LISTEN AND PRACTICE: *Rhythm patterns*

🎧 A. Listen to these words and phrases, and repeat them. Each pair has the same rhythm pattern. Mark stressed syllables (′).

Word	Phrase/Sentence
1. **a.** discóver	**b.** I met her.
2. **a.** bicycle	**b.** Talk to me.
3. **a.** development	**b.** in Canada
4. **a.** hospital	**b.** Open it.
5. **a.** America	**b.** She waved at me.
6. **a.** tomorrow	**b.** in April

B. Write the words and phrases from Part A under one of the rhythm/stress patterns below.

Rhythm/Stress Patterns

‿ ′ ‿   ‿ ′ ‿ ‿   ′ ‿ ‿

discover
_____   _____   _____

_____   _____   _____

_____   _____   _____

_____   _____   _____

---

4 **THOUGHT GROUPS AND DIFFERENCES IN MEANING**

A. First read the dialogues. Marc's lines are exactly the same, except for the way words are grouped together.

1. **a.** **Marc:** Did you see Tom?

   Alan: No, I didn't see Tom.

   b. **Marc:** Did you see, Tom?

   Tom: No, I didn't see anything.

2. **a.** **Marc:** Today at nine we're going to meet José.

   Maria: I've already met José.

   b. **Marc:** Today at nine we're going to meet, José.

   José: Sorry. I can't meet at nine.

3. a. **Marc:** There are two year-old children here.

   Maria: They're my sister's twins.

   b. **Marc:** There are two-year-old children here.

   Maria: How many?

4. a. **Marc:** I can't remember Alicia.

   Maria: You met Alicia last year.

   b. **Marc:** I can't remember, Alicia.

   Maria: You always forget.

5. a. **Marc:** I made three minute-long calls.

   Max: A minute isn't very long to talk.

   b. **Marc:** I made three-minute-long calls.

   Max: How many?

6. a. **Marc:** I think you know Milan.

   Alicia: Yes, I know Milan.

   b. **Marc:** I think you know, Milan.

   Milan: Yes, I've known for a long time.

B. Now listen to the dialogues in Part A and repeat them. Group words so the dialogues make sense.

C. Work with a partner. Practice the dialogues in Part A. Group words together correctly so your partner knows how to respond.

Harry Jackson called in sick to work today so that he could see a baseball game. He's just gotten home. He's listening to the messages on his answering machine.

A. Listen to Harry's messages.

B. Read the scrambled sentences in the box. Then listen to the messages again. Match subjects, verbs, and prepositional phrases to make sentences that summarize Harry's six messages.

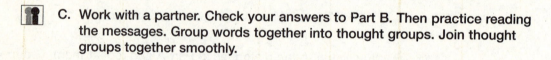

Subjects	Verbs	Prepositional phrases
Harry's wife	wants him to work	on Sunday.
Harry's coworker Al	won't be home	from Florida.
Harry's parents	will stop by	on Monday.
Harry's boss	are driving home	for dinner.
The cable repairman	will return his CDs	on Saturday.
Harry's friend Joe	postponed the meeting	until next week.

C. Work with a partner. Check your answers to Part B. Then practice reading the messages. Group words together into thought groups. Join thought groups together smoothly.

SELF-STUDY

First listen to:

- the dialogue in Exercise 1.
- the words and phrases in Exercise 3.

Now record them.

Then record Marc's lines from Exercise 4. Group words together so the responses are different.

INTRODUCTION

Important Words

In a sentence, one word is often more important than the other words. Highlight the most important word by pronouncing it with heavy stress on a high pitch.

We ⌢HAVE to move this weekend.   There's no other ⌢TIME.

Highlighting New Information

New information is often at the end of the sentence.

This is my ⌢SIS TER.

I found my ⌢K EYS.

Highlighting Contrasting Information

Pronounce words that contrast or correct information with strong stress and high pitch.

My name isn't ⌢SAM MY—it's ⌢SAN DY.

Highlighting Function Words

Function words are usually unstressed in a sentence. We can highlight them to emphasize their meaning.

A: Do you want soup or salad?
B: I want soup AND salad.

FOCUSED PRACTICE

1 LISTEN AND PRACTICE: *Highlighting important words*

A. Listen to these dialogues and repeat them. Circle the highlighted words.

1. **A:** I'm hungry. What's for dinner?

   B: Nothing. You didn't do the shopping.

2. **A:** My pictures were supposed to be ready today.

   B: I didn't tell you that.

3. **A:** It's hot in here.

   B: Open the window.

4. **A:** I'm sorry. That's my money you picked up.

   B: No, it's mine. I dropped it.

 B. Work with a partner. Practice reading the dialogues.

2 LISTEN FOR DIFFERENCES: *Hearing the most important word*

A. Listen to the sentences in column B and repeat them. Circle the highlighted words.

A	B
1. What did you lose?	**a.** I lost my keys yesterday.
When did you lose your keys?	**b.** I lost my keys yesterday.
Did you find your keys yesterday?	**c.** I lost my keys yesterday.
2. What kind of food don't you like?	**a.** I don't like French food.
You like French food?	**b.** I don't like French food.
You don't like French movies?	**c.** I don't like French food.
3. Who are you going with?	**a.** I'm going to a movie with Joe tonight.
Where are you going with Joe?	**b.** I'm going to a movie with Joe tonight.
You're going to a movie with Joe next week?	**c.** I'm going to a movie with Joe tonight.

B. Check your answers with a partner. Then create short dialogues by matching the questions with sentences *a, b,* or *c.* Practice the dialogues. Highlight the important words with heavy stress and high pitch.

> **EXAMPLE**
>
> **A:** What did you lose?
>
> **B:** I lost my KEYS yesterday.

3 | DIALOGUE

A. Listen to the dialogue and repeat the lines. Use high pitch and heavy stress to highlight the words in capital letters.

Chairman: May I have your ATTENTION, please. The planning committee has made some CHANGES. The party has been moved from THURSDAY night to FRIDAY night.

Assistant: Excuse me, sir. I THINK it's going to be on SATURDAY now.

Chairman: RIGHT you are, SATURDAY. It's going to start at NINE, NOT eight.

Assistant: Excuse me, sir. I THINK we decided eight-THIRTY.

Chairman: Oh yes, yes. QUITE right. And ONE last change. The party's going to be in the EAST Ballroom, NOT the West.

Assistant: Uh, no. We DIDN'T change the place. It's STILL in the West Ballroom.

 B. Work with a partner. Practice the dialogues.

4 | CORRECT ME IF I'M WRONG

 A. Work in groups of four or five. Read the sentences. In each sentence the underlined word is factually incorrect. Write the correct information. (You can check your answers on page 190.)

Russia **1.** Canada is the largest country in the world in area.

_____ **2.** Montana is the largest state in the United States in area.

_____ **3.** The Amazon River is the longest river in the world.

_____ **4.** The elephant is the largest mammal in the world.

_____ **5.** The buffalo is the largest land mammal in the world.

continued

_____ 6. The <u>Hudson River</u> is the longest river in the United States.

_____ 7. <u>Peru</u> is the largest country in South America.

_____ 8. <u>India</u> is the most populous country in the world.

_____ 9. <u>New York</u> is the most populous state in the United States.

 B. Read an incorrect sentence to your group. Someone in the group will correct your sentence. Use heavy stress and high pitch to highlight the correction.

> **EXAMPLE**
>
> **A:** Canada is the largest country in the world in area.
>
> **B:** No. RUSSIA is the largest.

5 YOU'VE GOT IT WRONG!

 Work with a partner. Student A will announce information about the class picnic, but some of the information is incorrect. Student B has the correct information and will correct Student A when necessary. Student A's information is on pages 192–193. Student B's information is on pages 195–196. Use heavy stress and high pitch to highlight words.

The picnic will be in . . .   Excuse me, but it's in . . .

Student A's information is on pages 192–193. Student B's information is on pages 195–196.

SELF-STUDY

🎧 **First listen to:**

• the dialogues in Exercise 1.

📼 **Now record them.**

Then record the corrections to the sentences in Exercise 4.

> **EXAMPLE**
>
> _CANADA_ isn't the largest country in the world in area. _RUSSIA_ is.

UNIT 33 Reduced words: *bacon 'n eggs*

INTRODUCTION

The function words *and, or,* and *can* have reduced pronunciations. The reduced pronunciations are standard English, not slang. You will understand English better if you are familiar with how these reduced words sound.

🎧 **Listen to how these reductions sound.**

And

And is pronounced [ən]. It sounds like the ending of *given* and joins to the preceding word. (Sometimes *and* is written *'n* to show its reduced pronunciation.)

bacon and eggs   bread and butter   paper and pencil

Or

Or is pronounced [ər], like the *-er* ending of *bigger*. *Or* joins to the preceding word.

soup or salad   right or wrong   rain or snow

Can

Can is pronounced [kən]/[kn] inside a sentence. It is unstressed and sounds like the last syllable of *chicken*. Reduced *can* joins closely to the surrounding words in the sentence.

Cho can cook chicken.   May can play the piano.
    [kn]   [kn]

Can't

Can't is stressed and pronounced [kænt], with a full vowel.

I can't do this homework.   We can't go.
    [kænt]   [kænt]

Short Answers

Stress *can* in short answers. Stress *can* if it is not followed by a verb. Use the full vowel [æ].

Yes, I can.   If I can, I'll go.
    [kæn]   [kæn]

Tip

If you stress *can* or pronounce it with the full vowel [æ], your listener may think you have said *can't*.

FOCUSED PRACTICE

1   LISTEN AND PRACTICE: *Phrases with* and *and* or

🎧 The single word and the underlined word have the same pronunciation. Listen to these words and phrases and repeat them.

1.	redden	red and white	7.	blacker	black or white
2.	deaden	dead and buried	8.	happier	happy or sad
3.	often*	off and on	9.	runner	run or walk
4.	fallen	fall and spring	10.	worker	work or play
5.	given	give and take	11.	buyer	buy or sell
6.	eaten	eat and drink	12.	cleaner	clean or dirty

*Most Americans do not pronounce the *t* in *often: offen*.

2   LISTEN FOR DIFFERENCES: *and* versus or

🎧 Listen to these phrases and fill in the blanks with *and* or *or*.

1. red _____ white   4. lunch _____ dinner

2. red _____ black   5. mother _____ father

3. come _____ go   6. land _____ sea

3   LISTEN AND PRACTICE: *Sentences with* can

🎧 The single word and the underlined words have the same or almost the same pronunciation. Listen to these words and sentences and repeat them.

1. weaken   We can go.   4. beacon   Bea can speak French.

2. awaken   A way can be found.   5. shaken   Shay can cook bacon.

3. bacon   Mr. Bay can come.   6. my token   My toe can bend.

Listen to these sentences and fill in the blanks with *can* or *can't*.

1. She _____ swim.

2. Juan _____ drive.

3. Don't call me if you

     _____ come.

4. Don't call me if you

     _____ come.

5. I _____ go this weekend.

6. I _____ bring it to you

     later.

5   **SOUNDS LIKE . . .**

A. Homophrases are two phrases that sound the same (or nearly the same) but have different meanings and spellings. Listen to these phrases.

1. a chicken egg   *a chick and egg* _____

2. Helen Heven   _____

3. blacker gray   _____

4. soak an eye   _____

5. the former meaning   _____

6. a customer habit   _____

B. Work with a partner. Think of another phrase with *and, or,* or *can* that sounds the same (or nearly the same) and write it in the blank. (You can check your answers on page 190). Practice saying the homophrases.

6 DIFFERENCES IN MEANING

 Work with a partner and take turns. Choose a phrase from the box. Make a sentence starting with *I can* or *I can't* and say it to your partner. Your partner will respond with *Great* if you say *I can,* or *That's too bad* if you say *I can't*. Pronounce *can* or *can't* correctly, so your partner knows how to respond. Look at the examples.

EXAMPLES

A: I *can* come to your party this Saturday.

   [kn]

B: Great!!

OR

A: I *can't* come to your party this Saturday.

   [kænt]

B: That's too bad.

come to your party this Saturday	lend you the money
give you a ride home tonight	teach you the tango tomorrow
fix your TV this weekend	pay your money back
teach you to swim this weekend	go to the beach this afternoon

7 SKILLS

A. Read the skills in the chart below. Check the ones you can do. Use the blank at the bottom of each section to add other skills.

Skills	You	Your partner
Practical Life Skills:		
drive	——	——
change a tire	——	——
type (using ten fingers)	——	——
cook	——	——
follow a map	——	——
use a computer	——	——
other _____	——	——

continued

Skills	You	Your partner
Athletic Skills		
swim	___	___
run a mile (1.5 kilometers)	___	___
do a flip	___	___
ride a horse	___	___
sail a boat	___	___
dunk a basketball	___	___
box	___	___
play soccer/baseball/etc.	___	___
other _____	___	___
Musical/Artistic Skills		
play the piano/violin/guitar/ drums, etc.	___	___
read music	___	___
dance (tango/ballroom/salsa/ ballet, etc.)	___	___
draw/paint landscapes	___	___
draw/paint portraits	___	___
sing	___	___
other _____	___	___

B. Work with a partner. Use *can/can't* to tell your partner which skills you can and can't do. Your partner will check the skills you can do on his or her chart. Pronounce *can/can't* correctly so your partner knows which skills to check. Then switch roles. Discuss your strengths and weaknesses with your partner.

First listen to:

- the words and phrases in Exercises 1 and 2.
- the words and sentences in Exercise 3.

▪▪ **Now record them.**

Then record eight sentences. In four sentences, name two skills you can do, joined with *and*. Use reduced pronunciations for *can* and *and*. Use this example.

EXAMPLE

I can *speak English* and *Chinese*.

  [kn]   [ən]

In four sentences, name two skills you can't do, joined with *or*. Stress *can't* and use the reduced pronunciation of *or*. Use this example.

EXAMPLE

I can't *drive* or *change a tire*.

  [kænt]   [ər]

UNIT 34 Contractions and reductions of verbs

INTRODUCTION

Contractions

Contractions will make your English sound more natural and "friendlier." Contractions are almost always used after pronouns.

am/is/are

I'm a student.
She's an artist.
John's an engineer.
You're late.
They're here.

have/has/had

I've already seen that.
Sue's lived here since May.
They've just arrived.
We'd never gone there.

would

I'd like French fries.
She'd rather drive.
If I were you, **I'd** do it.

will

I'll be at home.
You'll like the movie.
They'll be late.

not

That **isn't** right.
They **aren't** pleased.
They **weren't** clean.
She **won't** go.
I **wouldn't** do that if I were you.

Reductions

After nouns, many auxiliary verbs have reduced pronunciations. You should become familiar with how these reductions sound. If it is difficult for you to join words closely together, you should use the full forms after nouns.

- **Reduction of *are*.** When *are* follows a noun that ends in a consonant, it sounds like an *-er* ending and joins closely to the noun.

    You and Max are from Boston. (you and "maxer" from Boston)
    Ships are large boats. ("shipser" large boats)

continued

- **Reductions of *is* and *has*.** When *is* or *has* follows a noun ending in [s, z, ʃ, ʒ, tʃ, dʒ], it sounds like a long plural [əz] and joins closely to the noun.

> The rose is red. (the "rosəz" red)
> The church is beautiful. (the "churchəz" beautiful)
> Josh has gone home. ("joshəz" gone home)

- **Reduction of *have*.** When *have* follows a noun that ends in a consonant, it sounds like *of* ([əv]) and joins closely to the noun.

> The ships have sailed. (the "shipsəv" sailed)
> The painters have finished. (the "paintersəv" finished)

- **Reductions of *had* and *would*:** When *had* or *would* follows a noun that ends in a consonant, it is pronounced [əd] and joins closely to the noun.

> Dad would like chicken. ("daddəd" like chicken)
> Mark had better leave. ("markəd" better leave)

- **Reduction of *will*:** When *will* follows a noun that ends in a consonant, it is pronounced [əl], like the last two letters in *local*. It joins closely to the noun.

> The bank will close early. (the "bankəl" close early)
> Brad will take us. ("bradəl" take us)

Full Forms

Auxiliary verbs are not reduced in short answers or when they end a clause.

> Yes, I am. (~~Yes, I'm.~~)
> Yes, he is. (~~Yes, he's.~~)
> I will if you will. (~~I'll if you'll.~~)
> Would you like a ride? Yes, I would. (~~Yes, I'd.~~)

FOCUSED PRACTICE

| **I** | **LISTEN AND PRACTICE:** *Contractions* |

🎧 Listen to these sentences and repeat them. Use contractions.

1. I'm Íma.
2. You're Yúri.
3. They're thére.
4. He's Éaz.

5. We're wéird.
6. It's ítsy.
7. I'll álways trý.
8. We'd wéed the gárden if we cóuld.

A. Listen to the questions in column A and repeat them. Use rising intonation on the tag question (*isn't it?*). Then listen to the answers in column B and repeat them.

	A		**B**

A

1. Disney World's in Miami, isn't it?

2. The Statue of Liberty's in Washington, D.C., isn't it?

3. Fisherman's Wharf's in Los Angeles, isn't it?

4. The Liberty Bell's in Chicago, isn't it?

5. Harvard's in Boston, isn't it?

6. The Latin Quarter's in Seattle, isn't it?

7. The Sears Tower's in New York, isn't it?

8. The Pentagon's in Baltimore, isn't it?

9. The Space Needle's in Phoenix, isn't it?

10. The Alamo's in Houston, isn't it?

B

a. No, it isn't. It's in Philadelphia.

b. No, it isn't. It's in Orlando.

c. No, it isn't. It's in Seattle.

d. No, it isn't. It's in San Antonio.

e. No, it isn't. It's in Cambridge.

f. No, it isn't. It's in New Orleans.

g. No, it isn't. It's in Washington, D.C.

h. No, it isn't. It's in Chicago.

i. No, it isn't. It's in San Francisco.

j. No, it isn't. It's in New York.

B. Work in small groups. Match each question in column A with its answer in column B. (You can check your answers on page 190.) Read a question and choose a classmate to give the answer.

3 SOUNDS LIKE . . .

A. Homophrases are two phrases that sound the same (or nearly the same) but have different meanings and spellings. Listen to these phrases and repeat them.

1. The singers of "One Love"   *The singers have won love.*

2. Michael Wright _____

3. Lunches Served Here _____

4. His cattle* drink water. _____

5. Rose's herd* _____

6. The waitresses quit serving. _____

7. The disinterested groan* _____

*cattle: cows; *herd*: a group of animals; *groan*: a sound of displeasure

B. Work with a partner. Think of another phrase with a reduced or contracted verb that sounds the same (or nearly the same) and write it in the blank. Then practice saying the homophrases. (Hints: An -el/-le ending could be *will*; an -es ending could be *is* or *has*; an -ed ending could be *had*; you can check your answers on page 190.)

4 DIALOGUE

A. Jack Harper and Suzy Barolo have run into each other at their tenth-year high school reunion. Listen to the dialogue and repeat the lines.

Jack: Suzy? Suzy Barolo? It's Jack. Jack Harper. Do you remember me?

Suzy: Jack! How could I forget you? You look just the same—well, maybe a little less hair.

Jack: Oh, yeah—and a few more pounds! But you're exactly the same. How are you? What've you been doing?

Suzy: Well, I've been in Boise now for four years. I'm managing to support myself singing—some clubs and radio commercials. Nothing big yet. But I'm having a good time. What about you? What're you doing?

Jack: Well, Chris and I got married right after high school. We're living in Seattle. Chris's traveling now, so she couldn't be here. She's an event planner for the Sonics, and she travels a lot. . . .

Suzy: Sounds exciting. What about you?

Jack: Suzy! Is that Marta Simpson? She's lost a lot of weight. She looks great!

B. Work with a partner. Practice the dialogue.

A. Imagine that it is ten years from now and your class is having a reunion. What questions would you ask your classmates? What has your life been like during this time? Write questions to ask your classmates on the left side of the chart. Write information about your life in ten years on the right side.

Questions to ask your classmates	Your life in ten years
What will you be doing?	Personal life _____
_____	_____
_____	_____
_____	Job _____
_____	_____
_____	Other _____
_____	_____

 B. Work in small groups. Imagine that you are at the reunion. Interview members of your group about their lives. Use contractions when you can.

 SELF-STUDY

🎧 **First listen to:**

• the sentences in Exercise 1.

📼 **Now record them.**

Then record a one-minute description of how you think your life will be ten years from now. You can use information from the chart in Exercise 5 or add new information. Include some sentences with *will*, using contractions.

EXAMPLE

> I think I'll be married. I'll probably be living in . . .

Rhythm patterns of prepositions and particles

INTRODUCTION

Unstressed Prepositions

Short prepositions in prepositional phrases are not stressed.

in a mínute	to school	at níght
on tíme	for a year	with a fríend

Reduced Prepositions

Some short prepositions have reduced pronunciations. The reduced pronunciation is the normal pronunciation of these words.

at home	to the movies	for a while
[ət]	[tə]	[fər]

Of

Of is unstressed and pronounced [əv]. Before consonants, it is often pronounced [ə] and joins closely to the surrounding words.

> A cup of coffee (a "cuppə" coffee)
> A couple of friends (a "coupələ" friends)

Prepositions Used as Particles

When words like *to, on, in,* or *up* are used as adverbial particles, they are not reduced.

I want to.	Come on.	Go in.

Prepositions in Separable Two-Word Verbs

Stress prepositions when they are part of a separable two-word verb.

pick it úp	try it ón	throw it óut

To

To may be pronounced with the full vowel [uw] when the next word begins with an unstressed vowel. (When *to* is used as a preposition, it is unstressed even with the full vowel pronunciation.)

Full vowel: [uw]	**Reduced vowel:** [ə]
to a fríend	to the fríend
to anóther	to the óther
to enjóy	to gó
to agrée	to dó

FOCUSED PRACTICE

1 LISTEN AND PRACTICE: *Prepositional phrases*

Listen to these prepositional phrases and repeat them. Pronounce the words as one group. Don't stress the preposition.

1. at hóme
2. at tén
3. at the gým
4. on the wéekend
5. on tíme
6. on Mónday

7. for cláss
8. for stúdents
9. for a yéar
10. for dínner
11. to the párk
12. to a bánk

13. to schóol
14. in Téxas
15. in a mínute
16. in a húrry

2 IDIOMS AND EXPRESSIONS

A. Listen to the prepositional phrases in the box and repeat them.

for the time being	in a nutshell	at once	in a minute
in a jam	on the go	at noon	for good

Listen to these questions and repeat them. Join words together.

1. What's an idiom that means "immediately"? _____

2. When is the sun directly overhead? _____

3. What's an idiom that means "always active"? _____

4. What's an idiom that means "permanently"? _____

5. What's an idiom that means "now but possibly not later"?

   _____

6. What's an idiom that means "in trouble"? _____

7. What's an idiom that means "in summary" or "in a few words"?

   _____

8. It's 3:00 now. When will it be 3:01 (three-oh-one)? _____

C. Work with a partner. Practice asking and answering the questions in Part B. Answer the questions in Part B with a prepositional phrase from Part A.

3 LISTEN AND PRACTICE: *Stressed particles*

☊ Listen to these phrases and repeat them. Stress the particle and join words together.

1. finish up
2. come on
3. climbed up
4. hand it in
5. clean it up
6. turned it on
7. throw it out
8. go in
9. look out
10. go on
11. try it on
12. picked it up

4 LISTENING: *Americans and nutrition*

A. First read the passage. Unstressed words like articles, prepositions, conjunctions, auxiliary verbs, and pronouns go in the blanks. Fill in as many blanks as you can now.

How concerned are Americans about nutrition? What do they think about new trends _____ nutrition? The American Dietetic Association, _____ organization _____ nutrition professionals, wanted _____ know _____ answers _____ these questions. They conducted _____

nationwide survey _____ consumers, asking _____
about their attitudes toward food _____ nutrition.

_____ survey revealed three broad attitudes.

One attitude was: "_____ already doing _____."
People _____ this attitude _____ made major changes
_____ their eating habits _____ achieve
_____ healthier diet.

A second attitude was: "_____ know _____
should, but . . ." These people know what _____ healthy diet is
_____ believe _____ nutrition is important. But,
_____ one reason _____ another, they continue
_____ eat unhealthy foods.

_____ last attitude the study revealed was: "Don't bother
_____." These people _____ not concerned about
nutrition _____ have no desire _____ change
_____ way they eat. Some _____ these people
_____ well-informed about nutrition _____ others
_____ not.

B. Now listen to the passage in Part A. Check the words you've already filled in and fill in any remaining words. Then check your answers with a partner.

C. Work with a partner. The survey on nutritional attitudes showed that 40 percent of the consumers had one of the attitudes below, 32 percent had another, and 28 percent had the other. Which of the three attitudes do you think was most common (40%)? Next most common (32%)? Least common (28%)? Write the percentages in the blanks below. (You can check your answers on page 190.)

Attitudes	Percent
"I'm already doing it."	_____
"I know I should, but . . ."	_____
"Don't bother me."	_____

D. Work in small groups. Discuss the answers to these questions:

- Which of the attitudes toward nutrition is closest to your own?
- Do you think most people in your country have a healthy diet? Why or why not?

SELF-STUDY

🎧 **First listen to:**

- the phrases in Exercises 1 and 3.

📼 **Now record them.**

Then make a one-minute recording describing your attitude toward food and nutrition. Describe the kinds of foods you like to eat. Do you think they're healthy? Why or why not?

Rising intonation
Falling intonation

INTRODUCTION

Intonation and Pitch

Intonation is the melody of language, the pattern of high and low notes over phrases and sentences. Pitch is a single note on a word or syllable.

Intonation and Meaning

Intonation helps the listener understand what you mean and how you feel. Here are some uses of intonation:

- **Highlighting.** High pitch and heavy stress on a word tells your listener that the word is important. Pitch usually falls after the high note.

    I'm going to get married.

- **Final rising intonation is used to show:**

    1. You aren't sure about something. Final rising intonation is common with *Yes/No* questions.

        Do you have to work this weekend?   Are you hungry?

    2. You haven't finished speaking.

        I know . . .   (The speaker hasn't finished speaking.)

    3. You didn't hear.

        A: I have some news.

        B: What?

        A: I said, I have some news.

- **Final falling intonation is used to show:**

    1. You believe what you say is true. Final falling intonation is common with statements.

        There's a storm coming.

continued

2. You've finished speaking.

I know.

3. You need a specific piece of information. Final falling intonation is common with *Wh-* questions.

When is the concert?   (The speaker knows there is a concert but doesn't know when.)

- **Intonation with Lists.** Intonation usually rises on the first words in a list and falls on the last. The final fall tells the listener the list is finished. This intonation is common with phrases joined by *and* and *or*.

winter, spring, summer, and fall

- **Intonation with Tag Questions.** Intonation on tag questions can rise or fall.

1. Rising intonation shows that the speaker is not certain about the statement before the tag question (it is like a *Yes/No* question).

I haven't heard from him. He's OK, isn't he?
(The speaker uses rising intonation to show uncertainty.)

2. Falling intonation shows that the speaker believes the statement before the tag question is correct. The tag question is not asking for information, but for confirmation.

Look at that smile! You got the promotion, didn't you?
(The speaker believes the statement.)

FOCUSED PRACTICE

| **LISTEN AND PRACTICE:** *Rising and falling intonation*

A. Listen to the dialogue and repeat the lines. Follow the intonation lines.

Yoshi: What did you do this weekend?

Sara: I went beachcombing on Saturday.

Yoshi: Did you find anything interesting?

Sara: An old bottle, a big shell, and a sneaker.

Yoshi: Is any of it valuable?

Sara: I think the shell is. It's pretty, isn't it?

Yoshi: Yeah. What kind is it?

Sara: A conch shell.

B. Work with a partner. Practice reading the dialogue.

---

2   LISTEN FOR DIFFERENCES: *Hearing intonation*

A. Listen to the dialogue and repeat the lines. Draw intonation lines (╱ or ╲) to show the intonation on the tag questions.

Mei: You're not going to marry that horrible man, are you?

Lucy: I told you to stay out of my life, didn't I?

Mei: I've always supported your decisions in the past, haven't I?

Lucy: You're in love with him yourself, aren't you?

Mei: Your parents don't know about him, do they?

Lucy: You won't tell them, will you?

Mei: You're afraid they won't like him, aren't you?

Lucy: I don't know what to do. Do you?

B. Work with a partner. Practice the dialogue.

---

3   LISTS

A. Listen to these lists and repeat them. Pay attention to the intonation on the last word. If the speaker has finished the list, write *yes* in the blank. If the speaker hasn't finished, write *no*. Draw the intonation line over the last word in each list (╱ or ╲).

                                                  Finished?

1. January, February, March   *yes*

2. one, two, three   ____

3. knives, forks, spoons   ____

4. who, what, where, why   ____

5. at four o'clock, five o'clock, six o'clock   ____

continued

6. Angela, Mary, Susana   ____

7. third, fourth, fifth   ____

8. Friday, Saturday, Sunday   ____

 B. Work with a partner. Practice reading the lists. Use rising or falling intonation on the last word in each list. Your partner will tell you whether the list is finished.

4 DIALOGUE

Listen to the dialogue and repeat the lines. Follow the intonation lines.

Ray: Have you ever been to Daley's?

Susana: Yes, I've been there before. How about the College Inn?

Have you ever been there?

Ray: No, that's a possibility. But what about Michael's?

Have you ever eaten there?

Susana: No, that's another possibility. What about the Moon Café?

Have you eaten there?

Ray: Yeah. It's good, but I want to try something new.

Susana: OK, so we have two possibilities: the College Inn and Michael's.

Ray: The College Inn is a pizzeria and Michael's serves seafood.

Do you feel like pizza or seafood?

Susana: Seafood—definitely.

Work with a partner. You and your partner both want to go out to a new restaurant. You checked a restaurant guide and wrote down the names of six restaurants you've never been to. Your partner did the same.

Find out if your partner has been to any of the restaurants on your list. Cross off the restaurants that your partner has been to. When you know which restaurants are new for both of you, decide what kind of food you want. You can use the dialogue in Exercise 4 as a model. Student A's restaurants are on page 193. Student B's restaurants are on page 196.

🎧 **First listen to:**

- the dialogue in Exercise 1.

📼 **Now record it.**

Then make a short recording about a restaurant you like. Describe what you like about the restaurant (food, service, price, décor, location, etc.). Describe the food you've had there. Concentrate on using intonation correctly.

UNIT 37 Intonation: expressing feelings and attitudes

INTRODUCTION

Your intonation tells your listener if you are happy or sad, bored or excited, angry or pleased, certain or uncertain.

🎧 **Listen to how three people describe a movie they saw.**

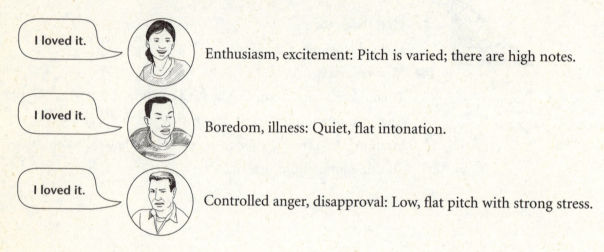

I loved it. — Enthusiasm, excitement: Pitch is varied; there are high notes.

I loved it. — Boredom, illness: Quiet, flat intonation.

I loved it. — Controlled anger, disapproval: Low, flat pitch with strong stress.

Tips

1. If you don't vary your intonation enough, you may sound bored or uninterested.
2. If your native language is Japanese or Spanish, you may need to expand your intonation range. Use higher high notes and lower low notes. English is a three-toned language; Japanese and Spanish are two-toned languages.

FOCUSED PRACTICE

1 LISTEN AND PRACTICE: *Listening for feelings*

A. Listen to the dialogue and repeat the lines. Use intonation to show how the speakers feel.

Mrs. Bevins:	Harry, that was Lucy on the phone.
Mr. Bevins:	Um-hm. How is she?
Mrs. Bevins:	Married.
Mr. Bevins:	That's nice.
Mrs. Bevins:	Harry, put down your newspaper. I said, Lucy's married.
Mr. Bevins:	Married? Who? When?
Mrs. Bevins:	Oh, Harry, I don't know. She said an actor. Or rather, a would-be actor.* She's in Las Vegas—you know she was going there for her vacation. She met him there. They got married last night.
Mr. Bevins:	In Las Vegas? An actor? He's not an Elvis impersonator, is he?

would-be actor: someone who hopes to be an actor

B. Work with a partner. Practice the dialogue.

2 FEELINGS AND ATTITUDES

Lucy and Max met each other in Las Vegas. They fell in love and got married the next night at the Tru Luv Chapel. On their way back to their new home in Los Angeles, they stopped for a day in San Francisco so Max could meet Lucy's parents.

A. Listen to the e-mail Lucy sent to her father after their visit.

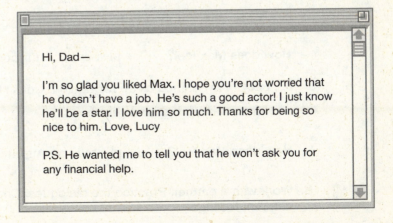

Hi, Dad—

I'm so glad you liked Max. I hope you're not worried that he doesn't have a job. He's such a good actor! I just know he'll be a star. I love him so much. Thanks for being so nice to him. Love, Lucy

P.S. He wanted me to tell you that he won't ask you for any financial help.

How does Lucy feel about Max? How does she think the visit with her parents went? How do you know?

 B. Listen to the e-mail Lucy's father sent to her.

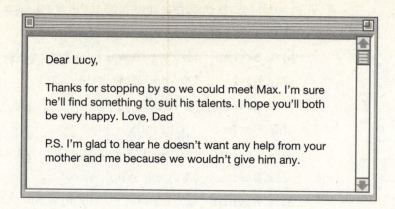

Dear Lucy,

Thanks for stopping by so we could meet Max. I'm sure he'll find something to suit his talents. I hope you'll both be very happy. Love, Dad

P.S. I'm glad to hear he doesn't want any help from your mother and me because we wouldn't give him any.

How does Lucy's father feel about Max? How do you know?

C. Work with a partner. Practice reading the e-mails. Use intonation to show your feelings.

3 INTONATION AND MEANING

A. Listen to the dialogues between Lucy and Max. Repeat the lines. Circle the word that describes how the last speaker feels.

1. **Max:** Bill and José are coming over to watch the game tonight.
   Lucy: Fine. It'll be nice to see them again.

   How does Lucy feel?   pleased   uninterested   angry

2. **Lucy:** You need to make an appointment to see the job counselor.
   Max: OK. I'll do it tomorrow.

   How does Max feel?   pleased   uninterested   angry

3. **Lucy:** I've signed us up for tango lessons at the dance studio.
   Max: Good. It sounds like fun.

   How does Max feel?   pleased   uninterested   angry

B. Work with a partner. Practice the dialogues. Change your voice to show different feelings.

4 SHOWING DISBELIEF

🎧 **A.** In the dialogues below, A is offering to do something for B. B believes A's offer is impossible. B uses high intonation to show her disbelief. Listen to the dialogues and repeat them.

1. **A:** Would you like to go to a steak house for dinner?

   B: You don't eat meat.

2. **A:** Can I help you with your calculus homework?

   B: You've never taken calculus.

3. **A:** Shall we go to a baseball game?

   B: You don't like sports.

👥 **B.** Work with a partner. Practice the dialogues. Follow the intonation lines.

👥 **C.** Now write a dialogue with your partner. A will make a suggestion or an offer. B will respond, showing disbelief.

   A: _____

   B: _____

5 DIALOGUES

🎧 **A.** Listen to the examples and repeat them.

> **EXAMPLES**
>
> **a. A:** Fruit is an unhealthy food.
>
>   **B:** Fruit!?   Disbelief
>
> **b. A:** What are apples?
>
>   **B:** Fruit.   Certainty
>
> **c. A:** I'm not sure what to have—something that isn't fattening.
>
>   **B:** Fruit?   Uncertainty

B. Work with a partner. Decide whether B's response shows disbelief, certainty, or uncertainty. Practice the dialogues, using appropriate intonation.

1. a. **A:** What language do most people in England speak?

   B: English.

   b. **A:** In the year 2050, what will the dominant language of the United States be?

   B: English?

   c. **A:** Half the people in Brazil will be native speakers of English in 2050.

   B: English!?

2. a. **A:** I put the sofa on the table.

   B: On the table!?

   b. **A:** Where did I leave my keys?

   B: I don't know. On the table?

   c. **A:** Where do you want me to put your books?

   B: On the table.

6 DIALOGUES

A. Listen to the dialogue and repeat the lines. Use the same intonation as the speakers on the recording.

A: What are you doing here?

B: I'm waiting for a bus.

A: The bus doesn't stop here.

B: No?

Now circle the words that describe how A feels about B:

friendly   surprised   suspicious   unfriendly

🎧 **B. Listen to the dialogue again and repeat the lines. Use the same intonation as the speakers on the recording.**

A: What are you doing here?

B: I'm waiting for a bus.

A: The bus doesn't stop here.

B: No?

Now circle the words that describe how A feels about B:

friendly   surprised   suspicious   unfriendly

 C. Work with a partner. Read the situations below. The dialogue in Part A takes place in both situations. Repeat the dialogue two ways to show the two situations.

1. A and B do not like each other at all. They do not hide their feelings.
2. A and B know each other and are friends. B is very disappointed to learn the bus doesn't stop here.

🎭 **D. Choose one of the situations from Part C. Read the dialogue with your partner to the class. Your class will decide which situation fits your reading.**

SELF-STUDY

🎧 **First listen to:**
- the e-mails in Exercise 2.

▪️▪️ **Now record them.**

Then write an e-mail from Lucy's mother to Lucy. How do you think Lucy's mother feels about Max and her daughter's Las Vegas marriage? Record the e-mail. Use intonation to show how Lucy's mother feels.

UNIT EXERCISE ANSWERS

UNIT 4

Exercise 4   Part D, Page 20

Bad luck: a black cat crossing your path, the bride and groom seeing each other before the wedding ceremony, the number 13, Friday the 13th, the number 4 in Japan, breaking a mirror, walking under a ladder

Good luck: carrying a rabbit's foot, knocking on wood, carrying a baby upstairs, being born on Sunday, finding a four-leaf clover, throwing salt over your left shoulder, carrying a silver dollar, finding a penny

Throwing the wedding bouquet: the person who catches it will be the next to be married

Throwing rice at the couple after the wedding: means the couple will have many children

Opening the doors and windows after a person's death: allows the dead person's spirit to escape

Wearing garlic around your neck: keeps vampires away

A howling dog: someone will die

UNIT 15

Exercise 8   Part C, Page 75

1. spiders   2. people and social situations   3. flying
4. open spaces   5. confined spaces   6. vomiting
7. heights (6 and 7 are tied)   8. cancer   9. thunderstorms
10. death (heart disease is tied with death)

UNIT 21

Exercise 5   Part C, Page 105

1. shopping   2. Outdoor activities   3. Going to museums and historical sites   4. going to the beach
5. attending cultural events   6. visiting national parks
7. going to theme parks   8. nightlife/dancing (7 and 8 are tied)   9. gambling   10. attending sports events

UNIT 23

Exercise 5   Part B, Page 113

1. Did you say "catch her"?   2. Is he coming?
3. Can he drive her?   4. Would he walk her cats?
5. all of her boots   6. The delays have cost her money.
7. The actress has left.

UNIT 25

Exercise 3   Page 121

1. "Breathes" is pronounced "breeze," with a long "z."
2. "Gifts" is pronounced [gɪfs].   3. "Guests" is pronounced "guess," with a long "s"; "arrived" cannot be simplified; "months" is pronounced [mənts].   4. "Asked" is pronounced "asst," with a long "s"; "answered" cannot be simplified.   5. "Rests" is pronounced "ress," with a long "s."

UNIT 32

Exercise 4   Part A, Pages 161–162

1. Russia   2. Alaska   3. the Nile River   4. the whale
5. the elephant   6. the Mississippi River   7. Brazil
8. China   9. California

UNIT 33

Exercise 5   Part B, Page 165

1. a chick and egg   2. hell and heaven   3. black or gray
4. so can I   5. the form or meaning   6. a custom or habit

UNIT 34

Exercise 2   Part B, Page 171

1. b   2. j   3. i   4. a   5. e   6. f   7. h   8. g   9. c   10. d

Exercise 3   Part B, Page 172

1. The singers have won love.   2. Mike will write.
3. Lunch is served here.   4. His cat will drink water.
5. Rose is/has heard.   6. The waitress has quit serving.
7. The disinterest had grown.

UNIT 35

Exercise 4   Part C, Page 177

I'm already doing it: 28%; I know I should but: 40%; Don't bother me: 32%

APPENDIX I: for team I players

UNIT 1

Exercise 5 Dictation
1. Look at the (ship/sheep) in the picture.
2. How do you spell ("pull"/"pool")?
3. Get some (paper/pepper) at the store.

UNIT 8

Exercise 6 Game: Vowels + *r*
1. What's the past tense of "hear"?
2. Where do you go to buy things?
3. What's the opposite of "finish"?
4. What's the opposite of "play"?
5. When two countries fight each other, there is _____.
6. What do people drive?
7. What's another word for "difficult"?
8. You enter a room through this opening.
9. What number follows twenty-nine?

Answers:
1. heard 2. (to a) store/(to) stores 3. start
4. work 5. war 6. cars 7. hard 8. (a) door
9. thirty

UNIT 11

Exercise 6 Fill in the Grid

	1	2	3	4
A	peace			raise
B	gum	peas		
C	back		race	
D	bag		come	

Ask your partner: What's in box *A2*?

UNIT 13

Exercise 4 Game: Past tense endings
1. listen 2. love 3. expect 4. need 5. play
6. drop 7. answer 8. fix 9. seem 10. arrest

UNIT 14

Exercise 4 Game: "TH" sounds
1. What's an unlucky number?
2. What's 10 × 3 (ten times three)?
3. What's the opposite of "unhealthy"?
4. How do you pronounce T-H-O-R-O-U-G-H?
5. If you're in California and you want to go to Washington State, do you go north or south?
6. What's the opposite of "fat"?
7. How much is 10 + 3 (ten plus three)?
8. On your hand you have four fingers and one _____.
9. What should you say when someone does something nice for you?
10. Is Los Angeles north or south of San Francisco?
11. Your parents include your _____ and your _____.

Answers:
1. thirteen 2. thirty 3. healthy 4. [θə́row]
5. north 6. thin 7. thirteen 8. thumb
9. thank you (or thanks) 10. south
11. mother, father

UNIT 15

Exercise 6 Game: [p], [b], [f], [v], and [w]
1. What's the name of the sixth letter of the alphabet?
2. What's the general name for foods like apples, pears, cherries, and strawberries?

3. What's the opposite of "sad"?

4. What's the name of the sport where tall people throw balls through a hoop?

5. Some people speak Spanish; some people speak English; some people speak Korean. Spanish, English, and Korean are _____.

6. What's the opposite of "hate"?

7. What's 50 + 5 (fifty plus five)?

8. What color do you get when you mix red and white together?

9. What's the opposite of "enemy"?

10. What's the superlative of "good"?

11. What number comes after ten?

12. What's the opposite of "small"?

Answers:

1. F [ɛf]   **2.** fruit   **3.** happy   **4.** basketball
5. languages   **6.** love   **7.** fifty-five   **8.** pink
9. friend   **10.** best   **11.** eleven   **12.** big

UNIT 16

Exercise 6 Fill in the Grid

	1	2	3	4
A		bus		buzzes
B	lacy	lazy		buzz
C			place	plays
D		places		

Ask your partner: What's in box _A1_?

UNIT 18

Exercise 3 Fill in the Grid

	1	2	3	4
A	catch		cash	
B	cheap	jeep		
C				joke
D		choice	choke	Joyce

Ask your partner: What's in box _B1_?

UNIT 26

Exercise 6 Fill in the Grid

	1	2	3	4
A	White House			white house
B	message	massage		
C	a dessert			
D		a desert	descent	decent

Ask your partner: What's in box _A2_?

UNIT 28

Exercise 7 When did it happen?

1. Ask Student B four questions about the dates in parentheses. Pronounce the date carefully. Use this question:

   What happened in _____?
   (1917, 1970, 1918, 1980)

2. Answer Student B's questions with this information:

   1914: World War I started.
   1940: Franklin Roosevelt was elected president for the third time.
   1916: Woodrow Wilson was elected president.
   1960: JFK was elected president.

UNIT 32

Exercise 5 You've got it wrong!
Tell Student B the information in the list below. Use these models.

   The picnic will be *in Riverside Park*.
   Ivana will bring *paper plates and napkins*.

Information

Place: Riverside Park
Date: Friday, April 28th
Time: Noon
Food and Drink:
   Ivana: Paper plates and napkins
   Goran: Soda

Ali: Chips and fruit
June: Pasta salad
Rafael: Cookies

UNIT 36

Exercise 5 Where shall we eat?

You and Student B both want to go to a new restaurant. Find out which restaurants Student B has been to, and cross them off your list. When you find out which restaurants are new for both of you, decide what kind of food you want. Use some of these questions:

Have you ever been to *the Tex Mex Grill?*

How about *Dominick's?* Have you ever been there?

Do you feel like *Italian food?*

You haven't been to these restaurants. Ask Student B if he or she has been to these:

Tex Mex Grill (Tex-Mex food)
Dominick's (Italian)
Ming's (Chinese)
Jackson's (soul food)
Beachfront Café (seafood)
The Student Prince (Russian)

You've been to these restaurants:

Samir's (Middle Eastern)
Deluxe Diner (steak house)
New Delhi Nights (Indian food)

APPENDIX II: for team 2 players

UNIT 1

Exercise 5 Dictation
1. Is that a picture of a (cop/cup)?
2. I want to (live/leave) quietly.
3. I have a (pain/pen) in my hand.

UNIT 8

Exercise 6 Game: Vowels + *r*
1. This is in your body. It pumps blood.
2. What do you stand on inside a building?
3. In baseball, what base comes after second base?
4. What's the name of the day you were born?
5. What's another word for "big"?
6. What's the opposite of "near"?
7. What animals fly?
8. What's the opposite of "less"?
9. What do you find in dictionaries?

Answers:
1. (the/your) heart   2. (the) floor   3. third (base)
4. birthday   5. large   6. far   7. birds   8. more
9. words

UNIT 11

Exercise 6 Fill in the Grid

	1	2	3	4
A		rice	rise	
B			have	pie
C		cap		cab
D		buy		half

Ask your partner: What's in box *A1*?

UNIT 13

Exercise 4 Game: Past tense endings
1. open   2. walk (the *l* is silent: *wa*l*k*)   3. help
4. suggest   5. count   6. move   7. change
8. like   9. practice   10. die

UNIT 14

Exercise 4 Game: "TH" sounds
1. Is New York City north or south of Boston?
2. What do you call the top part of the leg, above the knee?
3. The word "dead" is an adjective. What is the noun?
4. How much is 1,000 × 3 (one thousand times three)?
5. What's the name of the day after Wednesday?
6. If you're in New York and you want to go to Florida, do you go north or south?
7. How much is 12 + 1 (twelve plus one)?
8. What is the plural of "this"?
9. How do you pronounce T-H-O-U-G-H?
10. Where can you see a movie or a play?
11. Your mother's son is your _____.

Answers:
1. south   2. the thigh   3. death   4. three thousand   5. Thursday   6. south   7. thirteen
8. these   9. [ðow]   10. (in/at a) theater
11. brother

UNIT 15

Exercise 6 Game: [p], [b], [f], [v], and [w]
1. What's a common plural word used to refer to human beings?
2. What's 5 × 5 (five times five)?
3. You kiss with your _____.

4. What do people do in elections?
5. What's a word that means "not ever"?
6. Two common spices are salt and
   _____.
7. These animals live in water.
8. What's a synonym for "start"?
9. What's the opposite of "rude"?
10. What do the words *windy, rainy, sunny,* and *cloudy* describe?
11. These sea animals are the largest animals on earth.
12. You have these on your hands.

Answers:
1. people   2. twenty-five   3. lips   4. vote
5. never   6. pepper   7. fish (or whales, dolphins, octopi, etc.)   8. begin   9. polite   10. weather
11. whales   12. fingers

UNIT 16

Exercise 6 Fill in the Grid

	1	2	3	4
A	loose		buses	
B			loses	
C	price	lose		
D	prize		rice	rise

Ask your partner: What's in box *B1*?

UNIT 18

Exercise 3 Fill in the Grid

	1	2	3	4
A		Ed's		edge
B			H	age
C	watch	mush	much	
D	wash			

Ask your partner: What's in box *A1*?

UNIT 26

Exercise 6 Fill in the Grid

	1	2	3	4
A		blackboard	black board	
B			really	rely
C		mystic	darkroom	mistake
D	dark room			

Ask your partner: What's in box *A1*?

UNIT 28

Exercise 7 When did it happen?
1. Answer Student A's questions with this information:

   1917: JFK was born.
   1970: There were violent demonstrations in the United States against the Vietnam War.
   1918: World War I ended.
   1980: Ronald Reagan was elected president.

2. Ask Student A four questions about the dates in parentheses. Pronounce the dates carefully. Use this question:

   What happened in _____?
   (1914, 1940, 1916, 1960)

UNIT 32

Exercise 5 You've got it wrong!
Student A will give you information about the class picnic. Some of Student A's information is wrong. The information in your list below is correct. When Student A gives incorrect information, correct Student A, using this model.

   Excuse me, but *it's in CENTRAL Park*.

Correct Information
Place: Central Park
Date: Friday, April 28th
Time: 12:30

Food and Drink:
    Ivana: Paper plates and napkins
    Goran: Soda and juice
    Ali: Fruit
    June: Pasta salad
    Rafael: Cookies and chips

UNIT 36

Exercise 5 Where shall we eat?

You and Student A both want to go to a new restaurant. Find out which restaurants Student A has been to, and cross them off your list. When you find out which restaurants are new for both of you, decide what kind of food you want. Use some of these questions:

Have you ever been to *Samir's?*

How about *Ming's?* Have you ever been there?

Do you feel like *Indian food?*

You haven't been to these restaurants. Ask Student A if he or she has been to these:

Samir's (Middle Eastern)
Deluxe Diner (steak house)
Ming's (Chinese)
New Delhi Nights (Indian)
Tex Mex Grill (Tex-Mex food)
Dominick's (Italian)

You've been to these restaurants:

Jackson's (soul food)
The Student Prince (Russian)
Beachfront Café (seafood)